THE
SUGGESTION
BOOK

Notice on cover of Walton Heath's Suggestion Book

The COMPLAINTS Book
is in
The Secretary's Office

NOTICE

The Suggestion Book will now be kept behind the bar
and available therefore from the staff, who have been
instructed not to release the book to members who
have been drinking excessively.

John Bennett
Secretary

THE
SUGGESTION
BOOK

A COLLECTION OF SUGGESTIONS MADE BY
MEMBERS IN THEIR CLUBS' SUGGESTION BOOKS

COMPILED BY
DUNCAN FERGUSON & JOHN WILSON

ILLUSTRATIONS BY
JOHN RAYMER

FOREWORD BY
THE RT. HON. THE LORD DEEDES MC

AMBERLEY

This book is dedicated to all those golfers who wrote in their Club's Suggestion Book rather than airing their views to a relevant member of the Committee.

First published 2001
This edition published 2011

Amberley Publishing
Cirencester Road, Chalford
Stroud, Gloucestershire, GL6 8PE

www.amberleybooks.com

British Library Cataloguing in Publication Data.
A catalogue record for this book is available from the British Library.

ISBN 978-1-4456-0322-3

Typeset in Palatino.
Typesetting and Origination by Amberley Publishing.
Printed in Great Britain.

Contents

Acknowledgements

We are delighted that The Lord Deedes kindly agreed to contribute the Foreword.

We have many others to thank. The Golf Club Secretaries who willingly supplied material and, occasionally, cheerfully put up with our reminders, and the Captains and the Committees who supported their clubs' input.

We must also thank John Raymer whose drawings enliven these pages, and the Royal Ashdown Forest Golf Club for allowing us to include three of the cartoon sketches from their Centenary book.

There are many others, golfers, non-golfers and family, who have enthused about our project and who have given us the encouragement we needed.

To all these, our grateful thanks.

Preface

The idea for this book first occurred on a rainy afternoon whilst idly leafing through a noted Club's Suggestion Book. An early entry suggested that an additional Sunday newspaper be purchased for the benefit of some older members who liked to sit on the balcony which overlooked the course and read the paper – when available. The entry, its ink long since turned to sepia, received the terse reply "Trivial". It seemed that this simple suggestion and uncompromising rebuttal were so symptomatic of a bygone age with different values that they and similar reflections on the past should be preserved for the interest and amusement of a wider audience of present-day golfers.

Henry Longhurst, in his collection of short articles *Only on Sundays* may have felt the same when quoting the classic suggestion made by the late Lord Brabazon of Tara. His Lordship, who clearly felt that too little was being done to correct the waterlogged state of his course, wrote: "That the water in the bunkers at the 13th be changed."

Our research has been the greatest fun. We have received a large number of amusing, delightful and encouraging letters from the very many Golf Club Secretaries whom we approached. A surprising number of Clubs have either never had a Suggestion Book or, unhappily, have lost theirs. Others replied, "We used to keep one but it was only used for complaints!"

One of the best replies came from The Addington Golf Club. The Secretary/Manager, Bob Hill, wrote that the Club has never kept a Suggestion Book but that between the wars the story went round that the then Secretary, the great J F Abercromby who designed, built and ran the course, was approached by a newish member who asked for the Suggestion Book. "Aber" prodded the hapless man in the chest and replied, "I am the Suggestion Book!"

Suggestion Books provide a fascinating insight to social change over the years. For example, we no longer leave our bicycles in the Smoking Room, nor do we request that "the brake should meet the 9.30 a.m. train" and sadly the ubiquitous caddy has disappeared from all but a few well-known Clubs.

The book also shows how members' priorities have altered over the years. The price of a glass of port or the absence of writing nibs in the lounge seemed to be of major importance in the first third of the twentieth century, whereas today and perhaps more correctly it is matters such as handicaps, competitions, social events and the state of the greens that concern us.

Replies by the Committee, Captain or the Secretary to the suggestions are always quoted when available. We feel that this is a book for "browsers" rather than "readers" but hope that either will be amused by – and will possibly identify with – many of the entries.

But paraphrasing P G Wodehouse's Oldest Member, who, reaching for his glass of lemonade, might have said to the Young Man, "But I see you are impatient, so I will let you begin."

DUNCAN FERGUSON
JOHN WILSON

Foreword
by The Rt. Hon. The Lord Deedes MC

It was an inspired idea to bring together what golfers feel moved to enter in their Club's Suggestion Book. For it gives us insight into what goes through the Club golfer's mind. What will surprise the fair-minded reader of these gleanings is how many suggestions are sensible. I have always seen such books mainly as invitations to tease the Club's Secretary. Probably it is my perverse sense of humour, but the gems of this collection are those which seem to teeter on the borderline of sense and frivolity but are taken seriously by the Secretary or Committee.

Some years ago, there was a dispute on the first tee of a Kent Golf Club, which culminated in one golfer striking another over the head with his putter. I wrote to our Committee suggesting we put up a notice on our first tee: "This is a hard hat area." It was the solemn reply I received that made the joke.

There is a lot of social history salted away in these pages, as witness a member of my own Club, Littlestone, suggesting in August 1901 that "a better brand of Egyptian cigarettes be kept". No Club today has need of a room where members' chauffeurs can take their ease; and precious few retain caddy huts. Consider the entry in Royal Ashdown's book in August 1900, "that golf balls be on sale in the Club on the Sabbath". Or the protest of a West Hill member: "Why have we stopped sending wreaths when members die – surely a mistake?"

This is a book for social historians as well as golfers.

BILL DEEDES

The Clubs Included

Aldeburgh

Bearsted
Boyce Hill
Broadstone
Burhill

Chislehurst

Effingham
Epsom

Formby

Ganton

Hale
Halesowen
Hallowes
Hankley Common
Hayling
Helensburgh

Hindhead
Hunstanton
Huntercombe

Killarney
Knaresborough

Littlestone
Lundin

North Hants

Porters Park
Prestwick

Ranfurly Castle
Reigate Heath
Royal Ashdown Forest
Royal Cinque Ports
Royal Cromer
Royal Liverpool
Royal North Devon

Royal Norwich

Royal St George's

Royal West Norfolk

Royal Wimbledon

Runcorn

Rye

Saunton

Scarborough North Cliff

Seacroft

Seaford

Sunningdale

Tandridge

Tandridge Ladies

Temple

Thorpe Hall

Wallasey

Walton Heath

West Hill

Wilmslow

Woking

These Clubs comprise the Index at the end of the book.

The Course

Two early suggestions

October 1893. Would it not be an improvement to provide a curling pond when stress of weather prevents golf being played?

March 1895. The 6th tee has been under water for four days!! Isn't it time to change it?

Royal Ashdown Forest

Unplayable lies

27 December 1886. Two horses have been on 17th and 18th holes and obviously elsewhere. Propose immediate action to trace via local stables and/or police. We should bring charges, damage or trespass can be shown.

The incident is deplored by all members. Active steps are being taken to deal with the incident.

Hayling

Two comments on the state of the greens (which evoked no response)

That the greens be properly turfed.

That water be laid on to all the greens.

Reigate Heath

More relief sought

1908. That a boy be sent round the greens on Sunday mornings to remove sheep droppings. This would occupy very little time and would save much time to players on the greens.

Sunday labour not allowed on the links.

Wilmslow

20 members signed this suggestion, proving that the course once had some bunkers

That the 6th and 9th bunkers shall be filled with proper sand (sea) instead of "concrete" as at present.

Royal Ashdown Forest

One at a time, please

5 November 1899. That the bunker going to the 3rd hole be boarded up to prevent it spreading towards the hole.

That <u>one</u> member shall not make all the suggestions of the Club.

Hunstanton

Patience rewarded

1907. That the tees on the 7th be levelled.

This can best be done in the Autumn [year not stated...]

Note: This matter was raised again in 1923, and in 1952, which elicited an unsatisfactory reply. The problem was eventually dealt with several years later.

Sunningdale

An Escalator?

That a rolling staircase be provided from the 6th green to the 7th tee and an overhead wire with a trolley from the 7th tee to the 7th green.

Wilmslow

Putting speeds

5 August 1923. That the blades of the machines for mowing the putting greens be set higher. At present putting is a speculation.

The Green Committee are satisfied that the condition of the putting greens is quite satisfactory, and differs, as golfers would expect, from inland greens.

Rye

More about bunkers

I would suggest that the disreputable looking wet bunkers near the second green and elsewhere should have a foot or so of sand put in them so as to bring them above the water level.

Rye

A fishy solution

2 February 1975. That since the water in the bunker at the 11th hole is apparently to be a permanent feature, the Committee consider stocking it with trout.

Prestwick

Prompt response

18 June 1988. Since water is still cheap and plentiful, suggest that the greens staff put some in the ball washers.

Most ball washers had been filled the day previous but two had been missed. The omission was rectified within ½ an hour of this suggestion being made.

Hayling

1904. That a mowing machine be used instead of a scythe.

Noted.

Royal Cinque Ports

Flags requested

Suggested that the "flags" be used instead of the metal marking pins. The "flags" show up the position of the hole on the green so much better. Those now in use at Sandwich are a great success – going out red, white centre, coming home, white with red centre.

This suggestion is not approved by the Committee.

Members who hope the Committee will reconsider this decision are invited to sign their names here. [Only one signature.]

Royal Cinque Ports

Better late …

May 1911. Now that the roads have been satisfactorily attended to by the greenkeeper, may last year's footprints be removed from the bunkers.

Attended to.

Burhill

One from a possible sadist

20 December 1909. I suggest a bunker is made, *the whole width of the course*, at the first hole so as to catch a topped drive.

Formby

Clover and mushroom patches

29 July 1911. That great care should be taken never to put the hole, on any putting green, in the middle of a clover patch. There is always room for a hole on a piece of grass on this course *vide* 10th green today.

Noted.

Royal Cinque Ports

15 September 1999. Such a pity to mow the Mike Ologg mushrooms.

You may be assured there is definitely not a policy to mow mushrooms, but there is a policy to mow grass.

Rye

26 members supported this idea

14 September 1920. That the bush on the right of the 3rd green be removed.

The Directors will endeavour to meet the wishes of the members signing this suggestion.

11 March 1962. Ref the entry dated 14.9.20, it is noted that the bush still remains (despite the arsonistic efforts of one of the distinguished members).

Seacroft

Pitch marks – the eternal problem

7 June 2000. Have just played the loop with my daughter. The greens are in superb condition and a credit to the greenkeeper and his staff. If we, the members, do

not make an effort to repair pitch marks all their efforts will be wasted. I repaired ten (10!) on the first green alone.

The comment is welcomed, with thanks from the Board.

Huntercombe

Rabbits

23 December 1912. That the rabbit catcher on the links be stopped carrying a gun in any circumstances near the course. He again pointed his gun at three members teeing off on the 16th today from a distance of 40 or 50 yards.

Rabbit catcher? What were the members' handicaps please?

Seacroft

18 October 1931. If the rabbits are not required for the staff, they should be killed off.

Noted. Action has been taken.

Hunstanton

Stepladders needed

22 October 1914. That some attention be paid to the bunkers, and that they be raked over occasionally or if this is too costly a local rule be passed that you be allowed to drop out of holes over two feet deep.

Instructions have been given for this to be done.

Seacroft

While the sun shines ...

June 1923. That it is incredible that horse rakes are not used for gathering the hay, saving much labour and annoyance to members in searching for balls.

Considered by the Committee as being unsuitable.

Burhill

A cry from three lady members

10 October 1920. Could the barbed wire on the pin at the 6th hole be removed, as ladies have had dresses torn.

Hale

An original idea

21 October 1922. That a large yellow lemon be substituted for a flag at the 6th hole. With the afternoon sun and the green in the shade it is very difficult to see the flag at all at present when approaching.

Comment signed by three members: Why not three golden balls?

Wilmslow

15 Members wrote this

2 July 1967. Instead of aping Muirfield would it not be preferable to cut the rough NOW:

(a) to restore the character and appearance of the course
(b) to improve the enjoyment of the majority of members
(c) to speed up play

(d) to reduce the cost of playing golf
(e) to encourage visitors to come again
(f) to minimize the risk of hay fever
(g) before it's too late.

Hindhead

Boots are needed

3 March 1927. During the last week, the weather has been very wet. The horse attached to the big roller has been rolling the fairways at the 1st hole, 10th hole, 11th and 12th holes, and making deep hoof marks, thus doing more harm than good. Suggested that the horse be supplied with leather boots. If there are no boots in the possession of the Club then boots should be provided and used.

Rye

Strong words from a disgruntled member

August 1929. Emphatic attention is called to the suggestion registered (various dates) that the course is being mutilated without expert advice. The mutilation now in progress on the 12th is absolutely utterly and entirely an unnecessary and useless expense. What sort of shot in what sort of weather from what sort of player is it intended to deal with? At the same time at the same hole any sloppy epileptic could jerk his shot down the bank to the green without let or hindrance.

Anon.

Two suggestions in the 1920s at the same Club

That a fishing net on a long stick be placed by flooded bunker at 10th hole.

That some method of distinguishing the greens from the fairway be devised.

Wilmslow

World War II brought a *cri de coeur* from a member who had occasional problems with bunker shots

September 1944. Owing to the difficulty in purchasing new golf balls it is suggested that in event of a new ball having been played into a bunker the player may replace it with an old ball.

Royal Wimbledon

Advice on sandcastles

20 March 1928. If the Green Committee feel they really must play at "building castles and digging pits",

Saunton Sands would be the ideal place to do it. However, anywhere, except on the Saunton Golf Course.

Saunton

Let them safely graze

August 1927. That sheep be reinstated on the course. This morning my opponent lost 5 balls not far off the fairway.

Littlestone

Litter trouble

1927. Suggested that steps be taken to collect litter from the course, which is strewn with paper and other refuse some of which has lain there for years. The Green men might be encouraged each to keep the holes to which he attends in order. The basket on the sand box on the second teeing ground is inadequate for the purpose of holding paper. The accumulations of several days have recently blown out. I have handed the Secretary a piece of hosepipe on which my mashie pitch landed at the 11th hole this morning.

A new paper basket has been provided at the 2nd tee, and the Green men will be instructed to keep the course as free from litter as possible.

Rye

The British Flag

23 April 1934. Suggested:
1. If the British Flag (the Union Jack) is considered suitable for display on St George's Day, it should also be flown on 1st March and 30th November, and at half mast on 17th March!

2. That the caddies know their job as indifferently as ever, and that their habit of loafing away from teeing grounds is just as prevalent as when this complaint was previously made, and that this casts discredit on the Club.

Rye

Too close

That the fairways be given a rest from continual close shaves.

Rye

Call for ball washers

30 August 1938. That ball-cleaning apparatus be erected on each tee.

Rye

16 July 1994. That rather more attention be given to cleaning out the ball cleaners. One of my golf balls dropped to the bottom of the 7th and to retrieve it I had to remove brushes which when brought out spattered two of us with filth!

New ball washers are to be provided within the next few weeks.

Huntercombe

5 February 1995. Now that Huntercombe has a multitude of Bayco ball cleaners, the course is truly municipal (Naf?).

Huntercombe

Peace has broken out

2 March 1948. It is suggested that notices marked "WAR TIME" be removed from the notice boards, as we are no longer at war.

Runcorn

No go area

27 October 1993. Some skilled booby-trap builder (Vietnamese I suspect) has spiked the path between the 17th green and 18th tee with the most vicious set of spiked, almost invisible, stumps, guaranteed to break the back of buggies and trolleys. Now that he has had his fun, could they please be removed?

Every effort will be made to identify these obstacles, and a counter offensive mounted at the earliest opportunity.

Huntercombe

From a fair weather golfer

November 1945. As the weather in the northern hemisphere is slowly but surely deteriorating as the years go by, it is suggested that at the weekends an up to date met report be placed on the Club notice board.

Royal Wimbledon

Scoop the pool

16 December 1967. It is suggested that, as the Committee are against placing wire netting just beneath the water surface on the first hole's water hazard, they <u>do</u> ensure that a "scoop" is <u>always</u> present so that members may retrieve their balls. These valuable effects are expensive

enough as it is, so it is infuriating to have no means of retrieving the wayward sphere.

Noted. The Committee suggest an old ball be used or a start made at the second hole!

Royal Cinque Ports

A novel idea for preserving the course

6 September 1991. After 3 years of improving the lies on the fairways, we now have to lift the ball from the fairway and place it in the rough. May I suggest that the membership musters on the car park at 9 am on Saturday and Sunday mornings and take part in club swinging exercises (perhaps led by the Captain). This will eliminate any unnecessary wear on the course, altogether.

Wallasey

Thank you

12 September 1991. May I say how splendid the course has been to play on during these very dry weeks, and how cheerful and friendly the reception in the clubhouse after one's game has always been. My suggestion? Please on behalf of myself and, I am sure, of very many other members thank those responsible for making it such an agreeable Club.

Thank you.

Huntercombe

Soft spikes anticipated

29 October 1969. That the wearing of long spiked shoes which are so obviously causing damage to the greens be discouraged.

Rye

Move the clubhouse?

4 October 1970. Could the clubhouse be moved a little more to the left, to prevent shots at 18th pitching on the roof?

Whilst sympathising with this proposal the Board regret there is insufficient Club land in this direction to deal with a Baring hook.

Rye

So there!

2 March 1968. That the Committee pronounce publicly and categorically what is the purpose of the beautiful little trees planted behind the 3rd and 5th greens.

To grow into bigger trees.

Aldeburgh

Hopeful suggestion from a Broadstone member

20 December 1972. Broadstone Golf Club is a very pleasant environment but in my considered opinion it could be greatly improved by leaving all the downhills and making all the uphills level. Perhaps the Committee might like to deliberate this point.

Noted.

Broadstone

Short back & sides

16 June 1964. That the "whiskers" surrounding the bunkers be cut (thereby making it easier for the ball to go into the bunkers!)

It is hoped to get at the bunkers this week. Grass has grown very rapidly and the staff have been hard pressed to keep on the top side of it.

Broadstone

A plea from Royal Ashdown Forest members

March 1928. Despite efforts over the past 10 years to alter and improve the course, these have never succeeded. Nobody expects a Bishop to design a Cathedral yet nearly every golfer, especially if he's around the scratch mark, thinks he is capable of designing or altering a golf course. What is needed is an expert to design a scheme of improvement to be carried out gradually. Someone with a thoroughly sound practical experience with considerable artistic ability. Mr H Colt and Mr T Simpson are suggested.

Noted.

Royal Ashdown Forest

Sandy requests

11 April 1995. Is it possible to have some sand in the bunkers on the course?   [Anon.]

Would it be possible to renovate and put sand in the practice bunkers please.

Yes.

West Hill

Did this poem do the trick?

6 April 1968.
The post that marks the hole at the third
Is far too low – except for a bird
(Okay for an eagle
But not for a beagle)
Must I grow to ten feet tall
To see just where to hit my ball?
Please raise it high for this old fogy,
Just to help him get a bogey.

Awarded 10 out of 10 for poetry.

Aldeburgh

Another plea for a higher sign

10 April 1911. That a flagstaff, twice the height of the present one, be put in the hole on the 4th green.

There is a difficulty: the tearing out of the hole. If this can be overcome, the Committee will carry out the suggestion.

Reigate Heath

An unfavourable comparison

1990. Having been away for 10 years, am horrified about state of course.

Caused by drought of '89, failure of watering system and dry Spring of '90.

Tandridge

Another sandy request

15 September 1995. Why has the sand above the bunker on the 10th not been removed? Just curious. Oh, by the way, the broken rake on the 11th has been there for ages. I, of course, don't find myself actually in those bunkers, but I'm just curious.

The Secretary will deal with these matters.

Huntercombe

Plea for a practice net

5 October 1930. Could a practice net be put up. This innovation would be popular, both with serious golfers who wish to improve their drive, and with others who may wish on occasion to let off steam.

Seaford

... and upgraded facilities

11 December 1995. Why is it that whenever I seek to use the practice net there's always a wind blowing the net in my face and also the one at the side!! Perhaps I am not deeply religious and not getting Holy favour!! Seriously though couldn't the net be fixed by a few bricks or some other very cheap alternative. Anything to prevent the follow through of the club ending entangled in the net and a potentially damaged golfer.

Effingham

After the exhaustion of my car battery and subsequent curtailment of my night activities in the practice net, might I suggest the installation of an electric light bulb.

Seacroft

9 July 1976. Can something be done urgently about (a) the nets – they look like a police crime scene and (b) the slabs and weeds behind. What can visiting societies think?

Effingham

Two watery hazards

5 April 1977. That the new back tee at the 12th should not be used during the period of high tide – unless a raft and lifebelts are provided.

During periods of high tide the Ramsgate lifeboat will be alerted in case any of the younger members get out of their depth!

Royal St George's

5 February 1977. Despite the present financial pressures, would the new Supremo and his Junta consider the purchase of a gondola and boatman to ply his services across the 12th fairway.

This has been noted.

Hunstanton

Wishful thinking by a member

7 July 1983. The lake at the fifth today was so beautiful I suggest it might be made into a permanency.

This was also suggested by a member of the Farnham team. Not practicable.

Hindhead

Uphill work

12 June 1964. Would it be possible to ease the gradient of the walk from the 9th green to the clubhouse?

The Green Committee are already investigating what "steps" can be taken.

Hindhead

A few more moans

The Committee should try to uphold the original designs by H S Colt.

Yes – reason why Hawtree (golf course architect) was engaged to advise.

Tandridge

23 September 1993. I often use the lower green on the 4th. Why is the pin never there?

The Green Committee will be very pleased to accommodate the writer on occasions.

Huntercombe

Yesterday a groundsman asked me to stop chipping on the 6 hole course – saying it was for juniors. Today my brother who is 15 was asked to stop playing on it, saying it was for beginners. I've never seen anybody playing on it – who the hell's it for?

The groundsman was out of order to remonstrate with a member. However it is a six hole golf course for use by members, not a practice area.

Royal Cinque Ports

Self help

If the green staff are unable or unwilling to "tidy up" the course, perhaps the members should do it followed by a "happy hour" at the bar.

Satis eloquentiae, sapientiae parum. The Board has noted this suggestion.

West Hill

The Nelson touch

2 September 1963. I was never any good at croquet and am too old to learn now. Last Monday Nelson playing a good pitch and run shot straight at the flag from a little to the left of the 12th fairway went through one of the hoops and finished not far from the hole. On Wednesday I played a similar shot from a similar position, hit one of the hoops and stopped short. I see no sign of wear between the green and the left hand bunker at the 12th nor at the 2nd.

The hoops which have been placed at various greens on the instruction of the Green Committee are "a moveable obstruction" under the Rules of Golf. They may be removed and replaced after playing the shot!

Seacroft

A devil of a problem

21 May 1999. While it may be unusual to find traces of cloven hooves in the bunkers may I suggest the green staff are given standing orders to ensure all bunkers are raked before every competition.

I am afraid that even the most vigilant green staff cannot cater for sheep wandering on the course during the day. Unfortunately sheep do not know when a competition is on. Hopefully the problem has now been resolved by attention to the fencing.

Wilmslow

A reprimand for this suggestion ...

25 October 1986. There is a gravel pit next to the 13th green. Can the Committee consider having some sand put in and then we can call it a bunker.

The Committee is confident that when the cause of damage to this bunker has been discovered and removed, the green staff will restore the bunker to its original state. The Committee consider that sarcastic entries in the Suggestions Book are not helpful and would prefer that complaints about any aspect of the Club should be submitted to the appropriate Committee member.

Bearsted

Tall story

5 October 1963. With reference to the extracts of the minutes published on October 5th, to me it seems a waste of money to provide mirrors at the 6th and 14th tees. In the first instance a telescopic periscope for use with a large giraffe would be required and this may

raise objections from the RSPCA. And surely the steps at the 14th are entirely adequate.

Noted by the Committee.

Seacroft

Trouble from a bird

30 April 1978. May I suggest that the crow (usually on the 18th) be shot forthwith. It frequently turns up divots, is very bold and easy to approach.

The Committee understands that at least one member – armed with a high velocity gun – set out to exterminate Mr Crow. However, what do you do when the bird skips over to be patted on the head? Un-British and also unsporting to shoot. No action therefore but we are trying to obtain the date of birth and when anno domini could take over.

Hankley Common

A fallen golfer

2 September 1972. Could we not remove the rope surrounding the 8th tee – I tripped over it for the second time this morning. What purpose does it serve?

Posts and ropes are placed along the edges of a number of tees to prevent golfers from taking trolleys on to them. In the near future these are to be repaired or renewed by stronger posts – but gaps will be left leading to the tee, so that golfers with long spikes are less likely to "trip". If you fall over the gap, there must be only one reason!

Temple

A complaint by Mr E

9 March 1991. I suggest that the man responsible for the so called pin placement for to-day's medal competition must be the greatest sadist in the history of the game.

A conscious decision was taken by the Links Manager to choose the driest spots he could find following the more or less continuous rain on the previous two days. The Marquis de Sade does not appear in his family tree.

This failed to satisfy Mr E who then wrote:

In order to put into perspective the entry above, it is suggested that, when the Chairman of Green asked in the presence of other members "I take it your entry was put in as a joke, or was it because you had a bad round?" he was wrong on both counts. It was bona fide, and my score was 72 net. PS I am indebted to the Secretary for his assurances in relation to the Marquis de Sade's family tree. His title, by the way, was not "Marquis" but "Comte".

Royal Liverpool

Two climbing situations

16 May 1969. As granite is now being used extensively, would cramp-ons be acceptable footwear on the course? On the path from the 18th tee should golfers be roped together??

Could a little more consideration be given when siting temporary tees during future alterations to the course. The tee in reference being the 5th on the West course. Even Sherpa Tensing would have problems with the gradients!!

The Head Greenkeeper does the best he can. This particular area is a problem but if necessary improvements are to be carried out, some inconvenience has to be accepted during winter months.

Saunton

Raising one's hopes

It is suggested that the 17th tee be raised so that one can see the target!

Rye

For whom it tolls

1 July 1976. Should there be a bell on the 15th fairway?

No it would disturb the Secretary – another danger!

Temple

Touché

24 September 1976. It is suggested that the short rough through the green be short!!

This has been carried out.

Hunstanton

A spelling error?

19 April 1987. Rather than replace bear patches on greens with turf as at the 6th, would it be better to re-

seed with the same species of grass thus increasing the chances of consistency for putting?

Were they brown bear patches? If so the STRI recommends re-turfing with good quality turf

Hindhead

An excuse for the "yips"?

17 December 1992. The greens are not bad they are diabolical. To adjust handicaps upwards in these conditions when most of us are taking 45 or more putts per round is quite ridiculous. It's just not golf.

Please see the excellent returns by members in competitions.

Hayling

Tea time

August 1957. As the back tea of the 15th hole is now habitually used as the medal tea I suggest that the tiger post be removed and thus cease to cause alarm and despondency to terrified rabbits. Possibly a worthy tiger tea could be constructed further back.
Captain: 2/10.

Royal Ashdown Forest

A "put down"

5 March 1961. Now that Dr Beeching has been appointed Director-General of British Railways, at a salary of £24,000 per annum, would the Council kindly enquire of him by letter if a few old railway sleepers could be obtained to renew the level crossing on the railway at the crossover. Signed "Ibid".

Not a valid suggestion as no Mr Ibid appears on the Members' roll.

Lundin

Ball Pirates

October 1965. Can something be done about "golf ball pirates" who roam our course, please? Today, from the 8th tee, I drove into the semi-rough. On reaching the spot I was asked by one of those individuals if I wanted to buy my own ball back!!

It is not practical for the Club to take effective action. Members themselves must warn suspicious "pirates".

Helensburgh

The rakes' lack of progress

4 March 1978. Bunker rakes would be much appreciated.

The purchase of bunker rakes has been carefully considered by the Committee. Owing to the cost and the problem of vandals, it has been decided not to incur this additional expense. If players would smooth over their footmarks on leaving a sand hazard, this would greatly assist green staff and others.

Hankley Common

Course changes challenged

7 July 1974. Congratulations are in order to the Committee for having changed the 15th from a boring par 4 into a boring par 5. How about course changes being approved by the AGM in future?

Noted.

Temple

Drastic remedy required?

2 March 1988. Suggest the Committee consider whether to plant potatoes or cereal. Very soon you will not need a plough so much is the course being spoiled by Arnold Palmer lookalikes. These people, I guess, are also responsible for the potholes on the greens. Perhaps a Japanese solution would be appropriate for these "Gentlemen" i.e. take with them a bag of seed and sand to repair their mis-deeds.

This is a matter of concern to the Committee. Whilst birds undoubtedly remove some replaced divots they are not responsible for all the damage. Members are continually being reminded to replace divots and the possibility of repairing scars with sand and seed will be taken up with the Head Greenkeeper.

Bearsted

5 February 1995. Have rails upon which one can rest/ lean one's clubs at all the tees ever been considered? This would be particularly helpful in the winter months.

No.

Effingham

4 April 1983. May we suggest that the Hut adjacent to the 9th green be used for ladies, bridge and coffee mornings, on Sundays, between 12.00 and 2.30 pm.   The Guinnless Golfing Society.

This book is provided in order that constructive suggestions may be made for the benefit of all members.

Please do not waste the Committee's time on making flippant and totally irrelevant suggestions.

Royal Cinque Ports

Ideas for improvements to the course and surroundings

25 February 1969. Could the possibility of a croquet and/or bowling green again be seriously considered in future plans?

It wasn't. This suggestion suffered the same fate as did H L McN's equally creative one of 1932 when his proposal to make two hard tennis courts came to nothing even though he was on the Committee and had a seconder, with the availability of five years' credit.

Hindhead

28 July 1988. Would the appropriate persons consider replacing the trees between the 5th and 9th fairways with more mature trees. In fact some of the existing minute specimens are beyond salvation – i.e. DEAD! In addition, of the remainder that are still with us, the majority require new and more substantial stakes, and the kiss of life!

Hallowes

8 March 1992. May I suggest that on the right as you enter the main gates a bed of colourful rhododendrons would enhance the Club entrance.

Why not present them!

Effingham

It is suggested that the Captain's motor car be removed from the lake on the 13th.

Recovery of the car (which is not the Captain's) is the responsibility of the owner through his insurers.

Porters Park

14 August 1981. A way to raise £3000 every Christmas and improve the course at the same time – plant 3000 small Christmas trees about the course in groups. Each year thin out 1000 and plant 2000 more. Trees usually fetch £3 each and cost very little as saplings. Labour maintenance no different to any other trees on the course.

The Committee thank you for your suggestion but after consultation with the Course Manager at a full Committee meeting on February 17th it was decided that the scheme was not practical at the moment due to the present programme of work and staff commitments.

Bearsted

Why not convert the two grass tennis courts to a bowling green? There are members like me who for medical reasons can no longer play golf but could play bowls. In 14 years of membership I have never seen anyone playing on the grass courts.

The court is too small and it would be expensive.

Effingham

11 October 1993. That a syndicate of leading bankers be established to finance the purchase of the additional equipment which will be needed to fill the proposed new machinery palace.

Rye

If at first you don't succeed

29 April 1967. Steps should be taken to improve the quality of the practice green, which at present defeats description.

6 June 1975. Could some attempt be made to cut the grass on the practice ground. It is so long that it self defeats the purpose of its existence.

Prestwick

Water pressure

1991. Could the water tap on the 6th be made to work better, please – pressure turned up maybe? It is only ½ inch high when turned on.

This will be raised at the next Green Committee meeting.

Tandridge Ladies

Taking a sledge hammer

When Mahoney's Point course was under construction 1937–41, Lord Castlerosse suggested that a plane should be hired to drop bombs in order to create bunkers.

This suggestion was not approved.

Killarney

The Club House

Bigger towels

18 June 1895. Suggested that larger and rough towels be provided in place of the present pocket handkerchiefs.

As these are not being intended for bathing purposes, the size of the present towel is considered sufficient.
                                                    Royal Cinque Ports

An ongoing matter

8 July 1895. That a refrigerator be procured by next summer ... and lemons. [See entries dated July 1934 and February 1935 on page 62.]

                                                    Seaford

Royal Warrant

That the use of a portrait of his late Majesty King Edward VII as an advertisement for a firm of mineral waters in the Club is to be deprecated.

                                                    Porters Park

Various requests

August 1900. That golf balls be on sale in the club on the Sabbath.

Royal Ashdown Forest

March 1905. Might a few (feather) pipe cleaners be dispensed about the Smoking room?

Not considered desirable.

Why not?

Royal Ashdown Forest

Putting your foot down

14 June 1913. That the cockroaches be dealt with.

Formby

Trade description

16 December 1913. That, at least, in the winter months the taps on the basins in the dressing room with the word "hot" on them should act up to this description.

This will be attended to.

Aldeburgh

When coming in soaking wet and cold, is it unreasonable to expect hot water in the showers and the drying room warm?

In this event, demand exceeded supply.

Saunton

August 1986. I suggest that an effective drying room be provided but if this cannot be afforded, a clothes line should be erected so that players can dry their clothes.

The drying room requires to be cleared of old clothes etc. and a notice will be posted advising members accordingly. When this has been done the facility should operate effectively.

Anon.

A pencil that writes!

I beg to suggest that a pencil, which can be used for writing, might be attached to the notice board in order that members may enter their names on the starting list. In order to save any heavy expense I shall be pleased to present the *first* pencil.

We shall be pleased to receive the same.

Royal Ashdown Forest

Inaccurate reporting

October 1986. That the Club employ someone having legible handwriting and an elementary knowledge of arithmetic to send up the reports of competitions. Of late these have been masterpieces of profound inaccuracy.

Royal Ashdown Forest

Would the board consider bringing back the old light shades, either that or would eye shades be provided? It's far too bright in here (the men's bar).

Lower wattage (40w) bulbs are to be provided.

Hallowes

Roll on the ball-point pen

21 June 1921. Might I venture to suggest a new pen nib is provided.

Hale

8 November 1930. That a new nib be purchased for the Lounge pen on the 1st of each month (or year?)

New nib in place; and two and a half brace will be found waiting in the drawer (unless poachers have got at them). This should carry us through to 1935!

Seaford

1 September 1923. For three days (Aug 30th, 31st, and Sept. 1st) there have been no writing materials in the Smoke room. Might I suggest a little foresight should obviate a difficulty of this kind.

3 September 1923. Since my small grumble has been attended to, I beg to withdraw above suggestion.

Hunstanton

October 1961. What about some new furniture for the Smoking room? And some ink? [Pencil entry]

October 1963. There is no ink, no writing paper and the handles are off two drawers.

Royal Wimbledon

Weight watchers

3 March 1962. Suggested that a weighing machine in the men's changing room would be much appreciated by members.

Anon.

Indoor sports

A proposal for a ping pong table generated the reply "Under no circumstances whatever". Bridge was more favourably dealt with. It was agreed that it should be played in the Committee room, with stakes limited to a shilling per hundred.

Royal Wimbledon

25 December 1922. That cards and proper tables should be provided and card money at 6d per player be charged as is the custom in most Golf Clubs. This suggestion is put forward owing to the many complaints of members who have been unable to obtain decent cards especially on wet days.

Agreed.

Hunstanton

Entente Cordiale

That in view of the importance of keeping in touch with public opinion on the Continent, the Club subscribes to "La Vie Parisienne".

The Committee do not consider that the members of the Club are old enough to appreciate this class of journal.

Woking

4 September 1923. That the Barrograph in the Smoke room would be of more use to members if fitted with a chart, or if the supply of these be exhausted that a fresh supply of charts be obtained.

Hunstanton

1920. That the Club obtain a 1920 Michelin Guide.

The Committee understand that a Michelin Guide is for the use of motorists not golfers.

Wilmslow

Sensible suggestions please

June 1934. That the Suggestion Book be attended to and the suggestions answered.

This suggestion is considered frivolous.

Royal Ashdown Forest

September 1970. May I respectfully suggest that the Committee change the name of this book to "Complaints Book".

One hopes for constructive suggestions.

Helensburgh

January 1980. Gentlemen, a very few members continue to abuse this Suggestion Book. The latest abuse is the removal of pages 186–189 inclusive. Should this continue, the Committee will have little choice but to remove the book, amending bylaw 22 as necessary.

Footnote: A further abuse on page 193 in September 1980 caused this threat to be carried out.

Helensburgh

16 May 1985. That some notice be taken of suggestions in this book.

Unanswered.

Woking

23 March 1992. I suggest someone looks at the Suggestion Book. It is 8 months since the first entry!

We have. Comments noted.

Effingham

Is anybody there?

It is 1.02 p.m. There is no one in the office although it is all open and it says "The Secretary is in his office upstairs" but he isn't. IS ANYBODY THERE?

Effingham

Patience rewarded

22 June 1930. On revisiting the Club I am glad to find that my suggestion of 23 September 1894 has received attention.

Woking

Lack of combs

27 March 1971. May we be supplied with some combs in the washroom, please, even if they have to be secured with chains?

[This request was ignored.]

Hindhead

For mixed competition days

8 March 1925. It is suggested that owing to the idiosyncrasy of the weather that a gramophone or other sound-producing implement be provided so that members who do not wish to get wet while playing golf could enjoy the day whilst dancing.

Porters Park

1988. Would you please consider buying only "ozone friendly" hair sprays (e.g. Alberto V05 – aerosol or Boots – plastic containers)?

When restocking we will do this.

Tandridge Ladies

19 July 2000. Provision of a hair dryer in the men's locker room would be in keeping with this excellent course and clubhouse.

This will be provided.

a) What a good idea to have a hair dryer.
b) May I suggest the Club provides one or two lipsticks.

The Board feels it can pay little more than lip service to this suggestion.

Huntercombe

One Club's Suggestion Book was not available during the Great War. This was the first entry in 1919.

That the enormous collection of old coats, hats etc. be removed from the dressing room, as at present there is not a spare peg to hang anything on.

Seaford

3 December 1993. May I please suggest that notice boards are lowered a few inches so that those of us of shorter stature can read the top notices.

Rather than lower the notice boards the notices will be displayed as low as possible.

Huntercombe

After a major fire destroyed the previous clubhouse

The architect's report is unconvincing and a mistake might cause lasting inconvenience. We can hardly be expected to be lucky enough to have another fire.

The Committee regret such an observation in the suggestion book.

Footnote: The Club had a second fire in May 1999, when a blaze started in the kitchen area. Only very prompt action by the Professional saved the clubhouse from destruction again.

Tandridge

Too short

20 January 1951. Could one of the looking glasses in the changing room be lowered a little? My poor partner (who is also the smallest member of the Club) strained his achilles tendon, tip-toeing and straining to see the top of his head
[Added afterwards: Perhaps a stool or perch could be provided?]

This will be attended to: it is hoped that the necessary measures may be completed before the next, most welcome, visit of the embarrassed member.

Rye

11 September 1902. That a wooden lattice-platform 1 ½ inches high and of suitable width should be supplied in the lavatory to enable members of short status to obtain full use of the basins.

A small platform for one basin will be provided.

Royal Cinque Ports

27 March 1951. Suggested that the drying room – at present a waste of electricity – be rendered effective.

This matter was already in hand and has been dealt with.

Hunstanton

1 April 1987. Could we have a machine in our changing room for cleaning our balls? The date is not significant!

Enquiries are being made re a machine suitable for installation in the locker room. Meantime scrubbing brushes have been placed in the basins and perhaps for the time being you will continue using the "old fashioned" method.

Saunton

After hours

Sunday 7 September 1997 11.30 am: There can be no other golf club on this island whose bar is closed at this hour. Quite astonishing!

The Licensing Act 1964 (as amended) does not permit the bar to open before 12 noon on Sundays.

Huntercombe

Refrigerator and lemons again (see entry on page 51)

July 1934. That a refrigerator be procured by next summer ... and lemons.

One will be installed as soon as the financial position permits.

February 1935. In July 1934, that is 39 years later, the suggestion regarding the refrigerator was repeated with barren results. We are delighted to note however that LEMONS have become obtainable during this period of years – a striking example of the advance of civilisation and the financial progress of the Club.

Seaford

An eloquent appeal for better ablutions

I am proud to be a member of Hallowes G.C.; a Club of achievment and traditions that are the envy of most. Shame about the ablutions; my pride dissolves in shame when I pretend not to hear the comments of visitors. Two W.C.s! Two showers! One footbath! How has all this been accepted over the years by members who have applauded the "improvements" howsoever costly to the rest of the clubhouse. There's worse!! Stools. We have two wooden atrocities, copied from old etchings of a Dickensian wash house. I realise that I must be constructive so for starters 3 modern stools for the shower room and suitable stools for the locker room – say 4. I know about the problems of extending the ablution facilities – problems are meant to be solved, please go to it Gentlemen.

I have noted your comments and will discuss at the next House meeting. Hallowes

13 November 1999. In case it is thought that the shower problems have been solved, I have to report that Nos 1 and 2 (from the left) offered some stuttering flow before apparently seizing up almost completely; No 3 seemed OK; didn't try No 4.

The Board is most grateful for this helpful observation. Sadly we are only too well aware of the problems with the showers which are receiving constant attention.

Huntercombe

But in 1936, a rap over the knuckles for a suggestion

It is suggested that the Club is not called upon to act as advertising agent of railway companies without very adequate remuneration, and the exhibition, presumably with the Committee's acquiesence, of the pictorial productions on their behalf in the smoke room, does not credit the members with a very high degree of taste and culture. Incidentally, the disappearance from the wall of the portait of our first professional Mr Harry Vardon, which thinking members of the Club would regard as of historical interest or value, is surely to be deplored. It is suggested that this portrait be restored to its position, unless the Committee has sold it for any considerable sum, and that the said advertisements be removed notwithstanding any payment the Committee may have received from the Railway Company.

The Committee does not feel called upon to deal with observations framed in such a discourteous manner as the above.

Ganton

Another rebuke

June 1963. We suggest to the Committee that the clubmaster be instructed to view his catering responsibilities with a more pleasant and accommodating attitude. On arrival at the clubhouse on a stormy night we attempted to order four coffees at exactly two minutes past nine. We were met with the curt reply "You may not order after nine o'clock."

The Suggestion book must not be used for making personal complaints against any employee of the Club. The Committee therefore rejects the above.

Helensburgh

A poor and dingy place

The undersigned members feel that the facilities offered by our Club fall short of those of other Clubs in the area. e.g.

- Very poor pro's shop
- Very poor men's dressing room
- Very poor washing facilities/shower?
- Uncomfortable bar
- Dingy dining room

Why don't the Committee raise the money by using the collateral of the freehold and let's have some decent fixtures, fittings and service.

Proposals for redevelopment of club buildings and improvement of facilities in the clubhouse are under consideration by the Management Committee and details will be given in the annual report to be issued shortly.

Hindhead

Paper slippers

15 June 1968. In view of the increasing popularity of the showers, suggest the Committee considers providing paper slippers (commonly used in America) in the locker rooms.

[Suggestion from a Peer of the realm].

Prestwick

1 August 1946. To come into line with other well known Clubs it is proposed that a shower be fitted in the Gentlemen's cloakroom. It would appear that this could be located without difficulty in place of one of the Gentlemen's toilets.

We are in line but have no coal. Suggest that Mr Shinwell be approached.

Seacroft

A bit of a pane!

On 16 May I found one window in the clubhouse open in the smoking room, no other windows in the clubhouse open. One reason that the windows throughout the house are not kept perpetually open, whenever the weather permits, is because of the difficulty of opening them, for the windows are heavy. Could not cords and pulleys be fitted to all windows? *[Two months ago.]* An unfortunate member of the Committee at my instigation valiantly endeavoured to open a window in the dressing room – result a smashed finger nail!

Noted.

Royal Cinque Ports

An invisible clock

11 May 1999. The Crawford Benson clock. This has been demoted to a position behind the bar. Unless the bar shutters are removed it cannot be seen. At all other times and in the members' bar it is not possible to get the time. Can this clock/memento of a great chap be resighted. (If it were re-sited, then it might be! Ed.)

This has been done

Huntercombe

Newspapers, crosswords and magazines

That at least one newspaper be supplied in the mornings during Easter and other meetings.

Cannot be done without a special messenger. Papers should now be here soon after midday.

Hunstanton

November 1921. Will the Committee consider what steps can be taken to prevent members removing papers, periodicals and magazines from the drawing room?

September 1926. Books, magazines, and papers are continually removed from the drawing room.

October 1930. *Punch* … found it missing twice in ten days.

Royal Wimbledon

July 1937. That those members who indulge in the hobby of solving crossword puzzles should be requested to bring their own newspapers with them for that purpose and not use the Club papers to the inconvenience of other members who require them for reading and reference.

Royal Wimbledon

8 August 1981. Would the Committee consider taking out a subscription for the *Daily Telegraph* to be delivered to "AB's" house daily, to increase the possibility of this publication remaining on the premises.

I accept this entry is made with tongue in cheek. See Club Rule No 34.

Hayling

The missing chessmen

October 1936. The set of black and yellow chessmen belonging to the Club have disappeared since the close of last season. Could they be found please?

October 1938. That an enquiry be made as to the whereabouts of the Club chessboard, and that the member responsible for removing it from the drawing room be asked to return it immediately.

Royal Wimbledon

A fairly put point?

A Mrs C. asked that the notice board should be lowered to a position to where it could be read without the reader's dress being scorched by the fire ...

Royal Wimbledon

The saga of the missing balls

January 1930. That the three ancient balls in the case above the mantlepiece in the Drawing Room, wilfully overthrown by some sacrilegious hand, be restored to their rightful position.

October 1949. It is observed that the sacrilegious hand, dormant for many years, has struck again.

November 1956. It is to be regretted that the advent of card players to the Drawing Room has seemingly brought about another overthrow of our ancient golf balls in their glass case.

September 1967. In former years complaint by a member was justifiably laid against the overthrow of three ancient golf balls that had stood, possibly since the institution of the Club, on perches inside a glass case on the mantelpiece in the Drawing Room, and as a result such a sacrilegious act was quickly righted. Now both the glass case and the three ancient balls have entirely disappeared. Can they please be restored to their rightful and honoured positions in the clubhouse?

It is much regretted that the present whereabouts of the case and golf balls are unknown i.e. they are lost.

October 1967. Found.

Royal Wimbledon

Repairs and renewals

August 1952. I beg to suggest (for the fifth time in five years) that the main lounge be repainted – from ceiling (and including ceiling) to floor – and that the chocolate brown colour of the walls should be altered to a less depressing colour.

We have no hesitation in endorsing the above suggestion and would say that Mr X be asked to put forward his proposal to improve this very dull room. [5 members]

Royal Ashdown Forest

14 April 1959. In view of the result of the Boat Race, perhaps we may have a dark blue ceiling in the men's smoke room instead of light blue.

Porters Park

17 May 1978. Stair carpet should be renewed before a serious accident occurs.

This has been attended to.

19 October 1980. I suggest that it is time for a new stair carpet before there is a bad fall by someone.

Carpet already ordered and laid.

Tandridge Ladies

Lead kindly light

Can something be done about the changing room? It is cold, dark and dirty.

The gas fire will be lit daily, stronger bulbs are being used for the electric light, and a proper boot brush is being purchased for members' use.

Broadstone

The table turned

October 1968. It would enable members to read the Club notice board if the odd table under the notice board was removed. I have suggested this to Captains, Secretaries, and Committees for the past 13 or 14 years without success. Is this table a Holy Cow?

The Committee has decided that the table shall remain where it stands.

Royal Wimbledon

A prayer answered

I would like to suggest that the phone in the card room be lifted two feet as I find it makes my knees sore on long distant calls.

As you were on your knees, your request has been answered.

Saunton

November 1960. In view of the number of people using the lounge for cards, we would suggest that the Committee consider the installation of an extractor fan to help purify the air.

This suggestion is being considered by the Committee.

Halesowen

Matter of some relief

That the original lavatory paper be gone back to in place of the present cardboard and sandpaper supplied.

The matter will be reconsidered when the present stock is exhausted.

Royal Cinque Ports

Would it be possible to have some decent toilet roll holders that turn when paper is pulled?

The toilet roll holders were installed to avoid stealing of the toilet paper.

[We used to get caravanners and campers helping themselves.]

Saunton

Call for a barber

7 August 1970. That some form of quality hairdressing for gentlemen be made available in the changing rooms.

[Suggestion from the current Captain].

Prestwick

A cry from a displaced member

Having taken refuge in the clubhouse from the manic activities which take place at home from time to time in order to ensure that no speck of dust is allowed to settle for more than a few minutes, I do not expect to be driven out again by similar goings on here at 5.15 pm. Is nowhere sacred?

If the suggestion is that routine cleaning of the clubhouse should not take place during the evening in clubhouse opening hours, the Committee supports your comments.

North Hants

Too noisy

30 March 1974. Please can we have the tannoy system

excluded from the lavatories and bars or vice versa. This is neither a railway station nor airport.

As the great majority of telephone calls for members and visitors are taken by the female bar staff, the need for some communication with the men's changing room is obvious. Speakers are installed in various other places in the clubhouse, one or more of which can be used at the discretion of the operator. The staff have been instructed that the internal communication system is to be used only when necessary.

Walton Heath

I suggest that some billiard cues be provided and the old ones offered to the Haslemere Museum.

The cue has been taken and every effort will be bent to straighten the matter out.

Hindhead

If we all may make so bold
Our playing cards are getting old.
To cheer us all on Sunday night,
Some new cards would put us right.

Purchased.

Royal North Devon

A darts board saga

16 October 1976. The arbitrary removal of the darts board from the lounge has seriously interfered with the enjoyment of many regular members. We feel that the facilities of the Club should not be concentrated solely in the areas designed for short term drinking. We request the reinstatement of the darts board in its original position.

The Committee's well considered opinion, giving consideration to all members, is that the suitable site for the board would be the spike bar.

20 January 1978. We would wish the Committee to consider that a second darts board be placed in the lounge behind locked doors only to be opened when the Club is not in use for major functions. [9 signatories].

The Committee is working on this in conjunction with proposed alterations to the clubhouse.

9 May 1980. Can the Committee give consideration to installing a darts board in the lounge bar?

The Committee defers any decision until the spike bar position is clarified.

20 August 1985. Could we please have a new darts board and a stronger light?

Agreed. Arrangements in hand for new dart board and improved light.

Boyce Hill

A square peg ...

I know it might be difficult after all these years to make a change. Nevertheless could the Committee please consider replacing the plug in the footbath in the men's changing room with one that fits?

Seacroft

Message from the dungeon (in reflective mood):

Mirror mirror on the wall
The ground floor room has none at all
For those of us who still have hair
Please find a man to fix it there.

Agreed.

Ranfurly Castle

10 May 1980. That the hairbrushes supplied in the locker rooms and the lavatories are washed regularly.

22 December 1984. [By the same member as above]. Would it be possible to have the hairbrushes and combs cleaned more frequently.

Prestwick

29 November 1980. Could it be organised to fit a razor socket in the changing rooms? I have observed several visitors searching for one, as I have myself.

This will be done when the toilets are renovated. Meanwhile members would appreciate it if you could use a wet razor before coming into the bar.

Royal Cinque Ports

Non-U?

That the use of the word "TOILETS" to indicate the whereabouts of the wash-rooms is not in keeping with the traditions of the Club and that the words "WASH ROOMS" be substituted.

Prestwick

The ladies are locked out

10 September 1973. Will the Committee please give instructions that the outer door to the Ladies locker room is unlocked at a reasonable hour in the morning. It has been found locked as late as 11 a.m., causing inconvenience to the ladies.

Ladies locker room locked at 10.45 a.m.

Would the Committee please treat the above with the contempt it deserves? Is the walk through the main lounge too much for them?

Grow up! Ladies locker room locked at 3.40 p.m. Shall we bring clubs through the main lounge?

Comments of this nature are quite unacceptable.

Ranfurly Castle

Pleas for privacy

In order that male members may not be exposed or their handicaps revealed, can we not have some form of automatic door-closing device fitted to the external gent's locker room door?

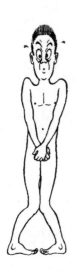

Sympathy and understanding were expressed by the Committee. However, the door closure has already been fitted.

Knaresborough

A simple suggestion?

16 December 1992. Buy a new clubhouse.

What a superb idea – a new clubhouse would be ideal. Perhaps the person who made the suggestion could sign his or her name, and also offer suggestions on the funding, location, design and timescale.

North Hants

In 1984 the gentlemen's locker room was extended by taking over a room which had previously been part of the steward's accommodation. This room looks directly out at ground level on to the practice putting green. It led to the following entry:

The occupant of locker 31 suggests that either a net curtain be put up in the window or lady members on the putting green be required to contribute an entertainment tax.

Wilmslow

Poetry pays off ... again !

23 January 1968.

Of one fact I am now quite certain.
The smoke room badly need a curtain.

I cannot drink while ladies watch.
It makes me coy and I slop my scotch.
Then sometimes when I take a nap
Upon the window they will tap,
Crying cooee, cooee or some broader jest,
So ruining my hard earned rest.
On Tuesday whilst taking tea,
Above the din of bacchanalian spree
I heard the words that froze my bone
He's here again – this time alone.
And fearing what they would do to me
I scampered home to sanctuary.
This I have set out the Committee to convince
That whatever else is wanted the priority is chintz.

The Committee wept over your sad plight
For they feel sure that you are right
One thing is absolutely certain
It is essential that you have a curtain.
And we will do our level best
To ensure you enjoy your rest.
We trust that in sleep you do not snore
For that really would be a bore.
We wish you sweet and pleasant dreams
Undisturbed by female screams.

Porters Park

7 May 1971. I suggest that lady members climbing the central staircase have too generous a view into the first men's changing room. (Not generous enough!!) (Spoil sport!!)

Agreed.

Seacroft

Unwelcome intruders

I would like to suggest that Bye Law No 6 be strictly enforced, particularly at weekends. Today there was a dog in the dining room at lunch time.

Royal Ashdown Forest

30 July 1896. That bicycles be not allowed in the Smoking room – there are two here now (1 pm).

Woking

14 January 1984. There has been a nail in the gulley of the third urinal from the end, for the past 4 weeks. In the high standards of the Club, it will have been cleaned and replaced daily. I suggest it is not replaced next time.

The continuing lavatorial vigilance and the perspicuous observations on the quality of cleanliness practised are much appreciated – especially, apparently, by the person who lost his screw. It's been collected.

Royal St George's

Three lemons again

It is suggested that the fruit machine, which continually and loudly makes the unpleasant "burping" noise, be modified to make a more pleasing sound.

Noted.

Royal North Devon

Noticed today that the gaming machine has been stolen! Would suggest an immediate investigation into clubhouse security! Have the Police been notified? I assume replacement is on order.

Not reported to Police in case they find it!

Ranfurly Castle

Having a quiet drink here is like absorbing moisture in a stamping mill. Could not the one-armed bandits be placed in a separate – and soundproof – compartment.

The machines are placed in the most advantageous place for revenue.

We came here for relaxation, not revenue!

Lundin

Suggestion (from some bald members)

13 December 1986. Some of us are in great need of a brush and comb in the locker room!

Prestwick

Difficulties for less supple members

Can we have some long shoe horns in the changing rooms? For the particular benefit of older members.

Royal Wimbledon

Tuning difficulties

18 September 1986. Having played a full morning's golf, I spent a good hour at the bar. We were somewhat disappointed at not being able to tune the rubber plant in, to watch a classic international golf tournament on television – i.e. we want our television back (please).

It is regretted that the TV was removed before the Suntory Classic, and Dunhill Cup at St Andrews. Every effort will be made to provide a TV set for all future golfing events.

Knaresborough

Mobile telephones

I regret to have to report the arrival at the Club of the mobile telephone culture. Last Wednesday three of these intrusive devices went off within twenty minutes in the Smokeroom. I believe that most members would find this unacceptable and would suggest that this use be prevented either by
(a) a circular letter to members from the Secretary, or
(b) empowering the Clubmaster and his staff to remind offending individuals of proper etiquette within our clubhouse.

The Board are in agreement with your feelings on mobile phones use in and around the clubhouse. This also includes the course and will be taking steps to inform all members of the Board's stand on this issue. Ranfurly Castle

Matters of dress

16 September 1964. That, before it is too late, the custom of tie and jacket be maintained for the bar lounge. (The entrance hall is otherwise available.)

Committee will investigate.

Seacroft

July 1965. We the undersigned suggest that the compulsory wearing of jackets by male members within the men's lounge is unreasonable. We feel that any reasonable casual wear as long as it is respectable is permissible.

As a reasonable standard of dress in the Club rooms is desirable no change in the existing rule is proposed.

Helensburgh

10 July 1998. Paper towels are as unwelcome at Rye as fourballs. Both are introduced by Americans. May we revert to more civilised materials.

Rye

Could we please perhaps purchase some good plain white china platters and plates for our lunches. The tin and plastic ones are very utilitarian and look remarkably like my dog bowls.

Rye

Something in the air

July 1968. We feel that the state of the gents' toilet leaves much to be desired. There is a most unpleasant smell and it is suggested that the use of disinfectant would be beneficial.

Clubmaster: Today was as sultry as could be. The above members were at the tail of a long field. If they would care to ask the Secretary he can tell them exactly how much is spent on disinfectant. The clubmaster will demonstrate how it is used.

Official reply: The Committee are looking into possible solutions.

Helensburgh

13th May 1989. May I suggest that the "funeral parlour/church music" is not appropriate background music for dinner. It drives my wife crazy (which is more than I do!) Something a bit more up to date would not be amiss.

To be discussed with the clubmaster.

Ranfurly Castle

January 1973. Are we too "square" to suggest jackets in the mixed lounge?

No you are not. The Committee will take action on this.

Helensburgh

Finally – a compliment

We are mere visitors to this splendid Club. We liked the course very much. But the real reason for this note is to remark on the beautiful display of flowers in the lounge and elsewhere. Whoever does them is to be greatly complimented. W J M, Sports Club, Bombay.

This is a unique appreciation, especially coming from visitors from India.

Hindhead

The Approaches

The train service threatened

14 January 1893. A Bill has been deposited with parliament for the amalgamation of the SE & EK Railways. If passed it will create a monopoly, and the inhabitants and visitors to Deal and Sandwich will probably suffer severely in the matter of fares, and number and speed of trains. I suggest that the Committee put themselves in communication with St George's GC with the view of urging upon the Town Councils of Deal and Sandwich, and the local boards of coal mines the urgent necessity of opposing the Bill unless certain clauses protecting us be inserted in it.

Royal Cinque Ports

Meeting the train

June 1907. That the brake meets the 9.30 a.m. train (at Walton-on-Thames) from London.

The 9.30 a.m. train from London is met by a brake on Saturdays and Sundays but the Committee regret that this is impossible on other days as the horses are employed on the course.

Burhill

3 December 1907. That the Committee consider the advisability of providing a light single horse wagonette for the use on days other than Saturdays and Sundays, in order to give one horse a rest and to run the pair wagonette on Sundays and further that the Committee consider the possibility of running the pair horse wagonette from the clubhouse to Newhaven on Sunday afternoon to catch the boat train (to London).

[Note: Seaford GC had a Dormy House for members resident in London who came down for the weekend and stayed at the Club – being ferried from the station by wagonette.]

Seaford

1906. That there be a train from Camber at 4.30 instead of 5 during the winter months.

Arranged, as suggested.

Rye

Early pleas for those wishing to swim

Could not a tent be erected adjacent to the clubhouse for the use of its members for bathing. If necessary a small charge could be made to bathers.

Left till next year.

That a tent be obtained for the use of members wishing to bathe. Tents can be obtained of Westley (Church Street) at 25/-.

Arrangements are in progress for the provision of a bathing hut or tent.

Hunstanton

Could a broom be placed in the bathing hut; as the floor sadly needs sweeping; likewise the seat. (A bather).

Unsigned suggestions cannot be considered by the Committee.

Hunstanton

Flying the flag

8 May 1895. Suggested that a flagstaff and flag be provided for the clubhouse for use on medals, Queen's' birthdays etc. Bristow Mast Makers, North Deal, can supply the mast at a very moderate rate.

Royal Cinque Ports

28 December 1929. I would suggest that the flag be hoisted on competition days – not only to remind

members who have mislaid their fixture cards, but also to remind others that serious golf is afoot.

Seaford

4 July 1980. Having regard to the high cost of replacement, it is suggested that the Club flag should be flown only on the occasion of Club matches, competitions or other special days.

During my tenure of office of Captain of this Club neither the standard of this Club nor the standard flag will be lowered.
Royal Cinque Ports

1 August 1990. Is it not time that the Club invested in a new quality flag befitting of our status in the County and further afield to replace the pathetic piece of rag which presently flies dejectedly from our mast on competition and other occasions. PS I'm thinking too of when it flies for me at half-mast.

A new flag has been ordered some time ago. We expect it any day. Can you hang on?
Seacroft

Odd requests

That the Committee provide two or more deck chairs.

This shall be done.

Hunstanton

25 January 1896. Suggested that some clean stable for horses, and shed to put carriages under, be provided for members driving to the links and further that some man should be in attendance to look after the same.
Royal Cinque Ports

1910. That better weather be provided.

[A day later] This has been attended to, temporarily.

[Same day] Many thanks – kindly persevere.
Royal West Norfolk

That some bathing towels be provided for the use of members.

Members must bring their own bathing towels.
Royal Cinque Ports

That the Club cat be renovated or peacefully retired.

Requis<u>cat</u> in pace.
Porters Park

The expression "fill your boots" is evident, and has been for many years, in the paving stones at the side of the clubhouse just after it has rained. A Society member filled his today. I ask that these stones be relaid to prevent rocking.

This is planned as part of the staff's winter programme.
Bearsted

That a bicycle foot pump be provided for the use of members.

Yes.
Hunstanton

12 April 1999. Could we please return to the selling of individual tees as one does not always wish to purchase 60p worth.

A frivolous suggestion.
Chislehurst

Room for chauffeurs

1912. Suggested that a room be provided for chauffeurs.

This suggestion was accepted by the Committee, and a room for chauffeurs was opened on 28 April 1913. [Note: Not being used by them, was converted into caddies centre June 1919.]

Rye

A cardinal cock-up?

I may be only a very Ordinary Seaman but I do know North from South! Aren't the four cardinal points on the weather vane the wrong way round?

The cost may be prohibitive but it will be looked into.

It is now exactly one year and the four cardinal points on the weather vane are still the wrong way round.

Various people and organisations have been approached without success, other than at prohibitive cost. It is not for want of trying that nothing has been done.

Aldeburgh

East is East and West is West
But a broken weather cock is not the best.
The eastern arm lies on the roof where it has been for over 12 months. Provide me with a ladder and I might put it up.

The Executive Committee very much appreciate your observation and kind offer. However, when a suitable access to the vane is provided, it will be retrieved/repaired in situ by another, to avoid any undue risk to your goodself.

Seacroft

1934. That a weather vane be erected on or near the clubhouse.

The Committee do not feel justified in spending the Club's money on such luxuries.
[In 1988, one was presented by a member and his wife.]

Tandridge

The price of golf balls

15 September 1922. The advertised price of Dunlop Maxfli balls is 2/6. Why are members of this Club still expected to pay 3/6 for them?

Give the pro a chance to read the paper.

Wilmslow

Tempus fugit

21 December 1975. Could the clubhouse clock be sychronised with the starter's watch on the 10th tee?

Porters Park

19 June 1978. Is it not time for steps to be taken to put the Club clock in order?

Now repaired but 5 MINS SLOW as at 0915 hours 30 June.

Royal Cinque Ports

1 May 1992. That the clock on the Pro's shop roof should be put right or removed.

Effingham

Other problems

3 May 1916. The kitchen chimney is out of plumb and should be seen by an expert. TCE.

This has been attended to.

Added on 1 April 1952: *A brand new one has been fixed – absolutely vertical. (Exors of TCE kindly note).*

Seacroft

5 December 1972. May I suggest that the nails on the starting board be replaced by right angled hooks. As things are, a strong wind is apt to blow the number plates off the board and across the tee to the considerable danger of anybody who is on it.

Agreed.

Royal Cinque Ports

1923. Whilst welcoming the energy and initiative in producing a New course indicator board on the caddie master's shed, it is suggested that a happier result might have been achieved had there been consultation with either the Council of Industrial Design or the Fine Arts Council.

Noted.

Sunningdale

No call yet for a 'phone at Deal

Suggested that the clubhouse be connected with Hunter's shop by means of a speaking tube or telephone or Marconi.

The Committee have decided to defer this matter for the present.

That the clubhouse be connected by telephone with Deal in order that members may be enabled to call for cabs. Possibly the cab proprietor would share the expense of the installation.

Not considered necessary. A cab can generally be got at the farm.

Telephonic communication urgently needed for many other reasons than the calling of cabs. Members of St George's are constantly wanting it and few would fail to find it a great convenience.

The Committee consider that this proposal should be more largely supported as it involves a considerable outlay.

Royal Cinque Ports

No response

26 December 1930. That the Committee consider taking some kind of official action regarding the attitude recently adopted by the Aldeburgh telephone exchange. Cases have occurred recently where the Steward has been unable to get the exchange to answer at all for as long as two hours. On other occasions the exchange have stated that there was no reply from the number required, which has afterwards, on enquiry, proved to be quite false.

Are attending to.

Aldeburgh

Cars and car parks

June 1906. That a motor shelter be put up.

May 1914. I suggest that the time has now arrived when the proposal to provide a motor shed should be carried out.

Littlestone

Suggest that only members with white painted number plates be allowed to park near the clubhouse.

Anon.

17 February 1914. Suggest that a shed or shelter should be provided for motor cars in the vicinity of the clubhouse. This would prevent damage to cars (particularly the tyres) on hot days.

This suggestion cannot be entertained at present as there is no available site.

Seacroft

4 April 1984. May I suggest that the car park be moved much closer to the clubhouse?

Yes – you may suggest this – but the answer from the Committee is NO!

Bearsted

20 June 1990. As we now have a car park reserved for staff, could course staff (including the Professional), please use it and not take up spaces in the members' car park.

Anon.

4 July 1975. If ladies are permitted into the Club at weekends, surely the Lady Captain and the Secretary could be permitted the use of their car parking spaces. It does look like discrimination to the newcomer or visitor.

7 July 1975. We have referred this to the Men's Committee.
27 July 1975. Not agreed.

Tandridge Ladies

Start 'em young

April 1969. On Good Friday there was a baby-in-arms on the verandah. Today there was a baby in a pram. Why is this permitted?

Royal Wimbledon

Members and Visitors

Mislaid members

16 June 1912. That a limited number of new members be admitted at a reduced entrance fee. There now seem to be very few regular playing members.

1 July 1912. Is it not possible that the above is due to the long grass all over the course?

Wilmslow

The Hun not An Hon?

21 September 1914. That the Committee consider the advisability or otherwise of retaining on the list of Honorary Members of this Club the name of an officer

in the German army who is at the present time fighting against this country.

The Committee regret the suggestion and do not propose to take any action in the matter.

It is surprising that the Committee should take no action on the above suggestion, and still more surprising that they should wait until a member had to protest in this book, and I hope their action will be censured at the General Meeting.

Royal Cinque Ports

Handicap questions

January 1924. That Club competitions would be more amusing if the Handicap Committee functioned occasionally.

See Rule XXI.

Royal Ashdown Forest

April 1931. There has been for some time a highly intelligent scheme exhibited in the Club, purporting to explain to members the rules on which the Handicapping Committee wisely limit the vagaries of their own mentality. These rules have recently been departed from in the case of certain aged and quite comfortably handicapped members. Why?

Seaford

24 December 1961. That the largest permissible handicap be increased from 18 to 24.

Rye

31 July 1961. That the Club become affiliated to the AAA and that Cridlaw JG be entered in the hammer event.

Chislehurst

Rule 19

11 October 1964. Having played 36 holes with Rev C, handicap 15 and having seen strokes played all day that any scratch golfer would be proud of, I would suggest that the Handicap Committee reduce his handicap to 9 on his match play prowess quite irrespective of any medal cards he recently presented!!

Seacroft

16 January 1964. May it please the Committee, I simply cannot afford to have Mr TGY playing off 10 handicap quite apart from which his proper handicap is 8. I therefore cannot see how he can possibly go up from 9 to 10!!! [HSC, JRM]
Neither can I. [MS]

While wishing to encourage Mr TGY to more successful endeavours in competitions (records suggest that success off a handicap of 8 has been elusive) the Committee are loath to involve Messrs. C, M & S in the risk of pecuniary loss to Mr Y in matches of less official standing. Therefore with the usual British flair for compromise Mr Ys' handicap has been amended to 9. He has been so advised officially.

Hindhead

Restriction on riveters etc.

11 June 1970. That societies of riveters and pipe operators, whose Articles of Association would appear to forbid them from dressing properly, or observing the etiquette governing behaviour on a golf course, be restricted to using the course on midweek evenings after 5.00 pm during the months of November, December and January.

Prestwick

Seen but not heard

29 November 1988. Would someone be kind enough to put up a notice asking the ladies to keep their voices down when playing round the course.

This will be mentioned at the Rules and Video meeting on 7th February.

Tandridge Ladies

4 July 1873. Could members perhaps refrain from shouting at their fellow members during the course of the golf stroke, and explain their grievance on its termination?

[Comment] The members are taking their golf too seriously.

Prestwick

Starting times

5 August 1985. It is a Wednesday morning 8 o'clock on the first tee. The air is filled with the joyous sound of excited chatter. Sprightly figures bounce to and fro, skittish as young goats, lively as lambs. There is a strange reflect light in the morning air, a kind of "false dawn" and in the background to the chatter, a prolonged hum of innumerable bees.

Who are these Druidic, early morning worshippers? You may well ask. A campaign for encouraging new junior members? A youth or school's tournament? No – this is the regular weekly meeting of the Veterans. The "false dawn" is the sun reflecting off their venerable silver hairs, and the hum of bees is the purring of their Power-Kaddies.

The point I would like to make (since there is a point to all this) is that such overcrowding occurs to the inconvenience of other members.

During my summer holidays (over now alas!) my fourball have had either to wait until this gathering of Veterans had cleared the 1st tee (as one visiting Society had to do on one occasion) or risk breaking the rules by going off the 10th tee. I am aware that the Veterans as full time members have a perfect right to organise their own private competitions and start when they like but may I suggest, very respectfully, that the Committee advise them that they do so often to the inconvenience of other members of the Club. I have some not inconsiderable support in making these comments.

We all enjoyed reading this! However, the serious side has to be considered. If you take as your starting point on any aspect of Bearsted GC life, that all members observe the same Rules of Golf for Etiquette and Club rules regarding starting tines – tees and reservations for visitors – then there is no problem!

The problem you so graphically describe results from the non-observation of one or more of these tenets. The tee is not reserved on the mornings you describe for any group of members.

Bearsted

Open all hours

22 November 1947. It is now eight years since I joined the Club. I am still without a key to my locker.

Porters Park

New Year Resolution

1 January 1976. May the course please be dyed green and may the movement of the ground be stopped before the next New Year's Day match.

Seaford

Slow Play

3 October 1970. It is suggested that Council advise those members who wish to take a leisurely stroll on Saturday mornings should not attempt to combine this hobby with playing golf. Three and a quarter hours for a medal round is ridiculous.

Lundin

9 December 1974. It is not reasonable to take well over 3 hours to play a single – and keep people waiting at every shot for twelve holes.

This book is for suggestions and not for comment.

Hunstanton

4 November 1984. The speed of play in the medal on Sunday was deplorable. Will the Committee please consider some action. It would help if Committee members themselves would keep up with play.

The Vice Captain will be looking at the situation and advising the Committee.

Bearsted

10 October 1992. For people busy during the week who want to play a friendly game at the weekend, I think the standard of play of some golfers is appalling. Having paid for a guest with a 6 handicap, we took four hours to go round behind two juniors who couldn't possibly have a handicap – couldn't weekend play be for competent golfers only?

The cry is "Fore"!!

Hindhead

Caddies

3 August 1893. Would it not be desirable for the caddies to have milk supplied to them instead of lemonade.

Royal Cinque Ports

1894. It be made a rule of the Club that parties playing with caddies may pass those carrying their own clubs.

Woking

October 1900. Suggest first class caddies be paid one shilling per round and second class caddies 9d.

Royal Ashdown Forest

10 March 1903. That caddies found not replacing divots when they are engaged carrying, should be suspended for a week or whatever length of time the Committee may think fit.

A notice to this effect will be posted in the Caddy House, and members are requested to assist the Committee in carrying it out.

Hunstanton

1910. I have been charged 2/8 for my caddy today. He was a small boy who did not know one club from another, never kept his eye on the ball and was apparently only 10 years old.

Regret that a mistake was made as the caddy master should only have charged 2/6. The boy in question had only recently come to the Club, and was in fact 14 years old.

Sunningdale

That boys who carry clubs here, but don't know one club from another, and whose idea of teeing one's ball is to press it into the middle of a handful of sand, should not be considered by the Professional to be 1st class caddies.

Not considered possible owing to lack of caddies.

Hunstanton

That a prize be offered to the caddies for smartness in the discharge of their duties – or some other plan be devised to bring about the same desirable result.

It would be difficult if not impracticable for the Committee to carry out this suggestion.

Hunstanton

5 December 1913. That following the practice of many other first class courses, caddies be allowed to play at certain times, when not required for carrying; the value of caddies being greatly enhanced.

Considered under the present circumstances impossible.

Seacroft

1931. Complaint about the too heavy clothing caddies now expected to carry. Suggest some limit be set (which might be of help to the 2.5 million unemployed).

Regret not possible to place limit on bag and contents. Would have to be adopted by whole golfing world.

Tandridge

1919. I suggest that there should be a daily boot parade for caddies on the grounds that the condition of the children's feet is distressing to the players.

The Committee do not feel that this idea is practical.

Sunningdale

1928. That players without caddies be allowed to go through.

We disagree with this revolutionary suggestion.

Tandridge

Suggest we have a card printed to give to all new caddies setting out five or six basic principles i.e. where to stand, replace divots etc etc.

Anon.

1935. That the caddy shelter be improved.

Brazier and benches already provided. Useless to provide tables as they are soon broken up.

Tandridge

Long hair

8 July 1989. As a thirteen year old at school, I was presented with a pair of scissors by the master and told my hair was touching my shirt collar. This was not acceptable. However I notice at this Club one G. McM promotes a hairline of shoulder length. Would the Captain please clarify "acceptable" hair length in this Club.

2 club lengths, stroke and distance.

Royal Cinque Ports

That the younger members of the club whose length of hair makes one question their sex either get it cut or refrain from using the gentlemen's changing room since considerable embarassment is caused to other members.

Rye

Sartorial notes

2 September 1927. That the Committee should post a notice which, I suggest, should read:
Gentlemen will not play in their shirt sleeves.

The Committee do not think it advisable to adopt this suggestion.

Aldeburgh

September 1932. I would like to suggest that Royal Ashdown Forest Golf Club should have a Club tie. [REC]

Mr REC is requested to suggest designs for the proposed tie.

April 1934. I believe that some months ago a Sub-Committee of one (Mr REC) was appointed by the General Committee to consider and submit for approval combinations of various colours suitable for a Club tie. May we be informed as to the results of the Sub-Committee's deliberations, and may we also be given an opportunity of inspecting Mr REC's multi-coloured combinations?

Considered and turned down.

Royal Ashdown Forest

30 August 1978. The "shirt sleeve order" notice on the lounge door is being ignored by many members (when it is not in place) and when it is reversed on the door, signifying normal dress, it is altered by anyone who cares to do so. I suggest that the notice should be held by a responsible member of the Club and that steps be taken to ensure that the Club rules are followed in this respect.

Noted. The position is rather difficult. The decision as to "shirt sleeve order" has been taken by the Captain or in his absence the Secretary but in the event of both being away on a fine day, well-meaning members have apparently taken action. The whole question of dress is under review.

Boyce Hill

8 January 1993. (Twelfth Night!) We the undersigned, having only had one pint, suggest we should have a Club bow tie.

February 1993. Bow ties have been ordered. Self tie will cost £5.50 each, ready tied will cost £3.75 each.

North Hants

12 October 1996. I think all members playing for the Club in matches should wear Club ties. It ought to be mandatory.

The decision to wear a Club tie is optional and each member makes his own choice. However, in 1997 et seq. all team sheets will have a sentence to encourage members of the team to wear a tie (or bow tie).

23 November 1966. Do we have to wear them when we are playing??

The Suggestion book is available for members to make sensible and helpful comments. If your entry is to count in this category, then the answer is that it is the individual member's choice to decide whether he wishes to wear a tie when playing golf. However, as you were one of the members who asked for the introduction of the Club bow tie, you may prefer to wear the bow tie.

North Hants

Monsoon weather

6 July 1993. The onset of the annual SW monsoon invariably coincides with the start of the Greenock Fair holiday. This being so, might it not be a good idea to change the date of the Anniversary competition?

The Anniversary competition is not played in Greenock.

Prestwick

A man's best friend

20 August 1933. That Mr Hunter's dog be destroyed. It attacked and bit me this evening at 6 pm. I was walking outside the shop when it rushed at me from the garden of the ladies clubhouse.

The suggestion book is reserved exclusively for the use of members of the Royal Cinque Ports Golf Club.

That the above suggestion is an unwarranted piece of impudence. This is a members' Club and most members possibly prefer the presence of the dog to that of the aggrieved visitor.

I heartily endorse the above.
It only showed the dog's bad taste.

Royal Cinque Ports

October 1964. May we suggest that dogs be no longer allowed on the course in any circumstances please?

Rule 54 (banning dogs) has now been restored.

November 1964. May I suggest that those people who abused the voting about dogs be the ones to be penalised, and NOT THOSE WHO DID NOT ABUSE IT. People who abide by the laws of the police are not sent to prison with those who err!!

The Committee regret this but the innocent have to suffer with the guilty. In view of the abuse of the privilege, there was no alternative but to restore Rule 54.

Broadstone

18 March 1973. Suggested that Cruft's Dog Show be held at Olympia in future and NOT on the fairways of Rye Golf Club. Five dogs with one match is too many.

I suggest people should get their facts right – four dogs!

Did they cause any inconvenience to others?

Yes – when we tread in it!! [A clean member].

As long as members keep their dogs under control they comply with By-Law 29. Numbers depend on members' discretion and personal complaints should be made to me.

Rye

26 August 1957. That the Club should present Mrs Parsons with a silent dog whistle.

To save expense, Anon should swipe the dog.

Aldeburgh

25 October 1998. In the case of a member knowingly bringing a bitch on heat on the course, that he be responsible for any ensuing reproduction. Can we have a ruling please.

It is the Board's view that Bye-law 19 adequately defines members' responsibilities.

Huntercombe

9 April 1985. We would like to make a further complaint against the gentleman who owns the 3 Jack Russell dogs on the 7th. Not only did the dog take the ball in play but also nipped my finger on trying to retrieve it.

Committee noted numerous representations had been made to this dog owner. Being rather aged it was felt the complaint had not registered. Matter to be kept under review.

Boyce Hill

"Love me, love my dog" the saying goes. But at the risk of making some human hackles rise, might I have the temerity to suggest that dogs which play on

Aldeburgh golf course should pay a green fee? They would then acquire the status of temporary members and could be required to conform to the etiquette of golf, one of the rules of which says that a player (in a bunker, at any rate) should remove all traces of his having been there. Then, by a local rule, the whole course could be designated a bunker as far as dogs were concerned.

Very nicely put. If owners do not observe the Rules, and exercise much stricter control over their dogs the Committee may have no alternative but to ban dogs altogether.

Aldeburgh

The dog situation on the course at weekends has now reached epidemic proportions. If owners are unable to train their dogs so that they stay with the match in which their owner is participating, may I suggest that they should be kept on a lead. Yesterday, play in my game was interrupted by a case of rape on the 3rd green, indecent assault on the 12th and a damn good fight on the 15th. As far as I know none of the dogs had paid a green fee.

Well-behaved dogs have always been welcome except on competition days. Poorly behaved or immoral ones should be reported to the Secretary.

Royal St George's

Miscellaneous

February 1935. That for the benefit of those golfers who hit their tee shots with a shade of fade, an implement be provided for retrieving golf balls from the pond at the 13th.

Royal Wimbledon

18 October 1936. That in the year 1937 members compete for the Coronation Challenge Bowl on the day of the coronation of King Edward VIII.

The Coronation Challenge Bowl will be played for on the day suggested. [Presumably it was, although the coronation did not happen.]

Seacroft

A question of chivalry and sport

20 May 1922. That except very occasionally for exhibition purposes (and then principally for the purpose of showing the impossibilty of arriving at a common handicap) the pitting against one another of players of opposite sexes is detrimental to the interests of both chivalry and sport.

27 May 1922. That (on the contrary but with due respect) this subject is rather for consideration and recommendation on the part of the Committee, and that in any case it would have been contrary to the interests of both chivalry and sport (and so forth) to bring it up at the Annual General Meeting while a contest of the nature referred to was in course of decision.

Current note by Secretary: This clearly caused quite a row. There is no immediate reply apart from a suggestion that a General Meeting be called.

Chislehurst

Members' rights

31 July 1977. We were surprised to see a 5 day member in the Club house and using the putting green today, Sunday 31st July. Is this in order?

Footnote: I presume that the above remarks have arisen by the fact that I (a 5 day member) was lunching in the Club yesterday. I always understood that the Club and its environs were permitted to be used by 5 day members as a privilege rather than a right. If this is not so, I would like a ruling on the matter. Anyhow, I was lunching with my wife (a social member) as her guest, and I played one round on a practically empty putting course with a full member as his guest. Ought he to have paid a putting green fee?

The 5 day member who has commented on Colonel H's suggestion is correct in thinking that at present 5 day members are permitted, as a privilege and not a right, to use the clubhouse facilities at week-ends. This decision was taken by the Committee four years ago, on revenue-earnings grounds, with the reservation that the privilege might have to be withdrawn if it became an inconvenience to full members.

In this case the 5 day member was doubly in order in lunching in the Club:

a) because of the relaxation mentioned above, and

b) because he was there as the guest of his wife, who as a social member, is entitled to use the clubhouse seven days a week.

Since the putting green is part of the course and not of the clubhouse, the relaxation mentioned above does not apply to it. However this seems to the Committee to be case of "de minimis non curat lex".

In fact, the 5 day member who has written his explanation above was not the member whom Colonel H and his cosignatory had in mind. But, having already aired its Latin, the Committee refrains from airing its French by quoting the maxim which begins "qui s'excuse..."!

Walton Heath

October 1936. That the Committee uses its discretionary powers to place on the notice board something to the effect that a member who does a hole in one shall not be expected to buy a drink for everyone in the bar, but shall for the rest of the day be the guest of the Club. This will stop a sentimental burden on persons who cannot possibly afford it and, on the whole, will be against, rather than for, any excessive alcoholic consumption.

Seaford

The Captain

18 January 1953. It is suggested that in accordance with the tradition the Captain's photograph not having appeared in the bar prior to 31 December 1952, all drinks served in the bar should hereafter be charged to the Captain's account until such time as the photo appears.

An objection has been received from the official receiver.

Porters Park

6 December 1959. That the Captain of Seacroft Golf Club bins his refuse in a more appropriate place than the 18th fairway.

Noted by the Captain.

Seacroft

19 February 1972. It is normal practice at other Golf Clubs to give the Captain priority on the tee for obvious reasons. It is therefore suggested that this Club adopt this normal courtesy forthwith.

It would be appreciated if all members respect the Rules of Golf.

Walton Heath

Something for the more mature member

5 September 1993. Suggest a weekday competition on a regular basis for the over sixties (18 holes) and for over seventies a competition of fewer than 18 holes.

Anon.

11 June 1950. Suggest Veterans Cup for our over 60s.

Green Committee recommend age limit 55 years, commencing 1951.

20 June 1950. We oppose above. We do not intend this Club is messed about by a lot of old men.

[Note: Veteran Cup competitions commenced in 1980!]

Seacroft

High finance

September 1976. May I respectfully request that the Committee reconsider the 75p charge for members' guests. In my opinion this is a gross over-charge.

The Committee have agreed to reduce all guests of members to 50p.

Helensburgh

Strong language

July 1956. I suggest that something is done to correct the swearing that takes place in the clubhouse and on the course. I think I am justified in writing that one hears enough of this sort of thing without paying £6.50 to hear it on the golf course.

The Committee have agreed to take steps to rectify this complaint.

Helensburgh

7 July 1998. With three societies in one day, can we expect a reduction in the subscriptions in 1999?

The exceptional day with maximum permitted numbers turning up in the respective societies caused some inconvenience to members. Such days are extremely rare and should not be allowed to raise false hopes of a reduction in subscriptions next year.

Huntercombe

7 April 1973. If VAT at 10% is added to the former entrance fee of 15p the amount is 1.5p. Why the 25p?

The prize fund has been losing money for some considerable time, mainly because the entry fees for monthly competitions are insufficient to cover the cost of prizes.

Walton Heath

Decisions on the Rules of Golf

That the player should stand over the rabbit hole (from which he picks his ball without penalty) when he drops the ball, and if he cannot do so (the rabbit hole may be under a gorse bush) he shall be penalised one stroke.

Reigate Heath

A case for 'L' plates?

In view of the crash at the 4th hole on Wednesday 20th June last, it is suggested that members using the electric caddy cart be required to wear crash helmets.

The Committee note this suggestion.

Hunstanton

Let's dance

May I suggest that we try to cater for the YOUNGER members by having music on a Saturday evening to which they could dance. This Club seems to die over the weekends and the younger members go elsewhere for their fun. We need an ACTIVE Social Committee to get things moving which should benefit the Club.

[No action was taken – no benefit or fun was anticipated from such intrusion.]

Hindhead

Making a splash

We suggest that D R W be banned from the use of the soda syphon for six months after soaking everybody at the Brassey dinner.

Approved.

Propose the sentence be extended for a period of 5 years or life whichever is the longer.

Royal Cinque Ports

A heartfelt protest

Why have we stopped sending wreaths when members die – surely a mistake?

It was an oversight that a wreath was not sent on behalf of the Club for the recent funeral of Mr X but rest in peace that suitable condolences will continue to be offered for the unfortunate in the future.

West Hill

Spelling B

31 October 1988. Any chance of educating our members in basic spelling? (See Course improvements) BEECH not BEACH. By the way, I have in my garden a 2 ft oak sapling, which is readily available to the Club if required.

Perhaps the suggested lessons could incorporate "Reading" as the comment was written in the Answers page! Thank you for the offer of the sapling.

Bearsted

A desperate measure

I second S D's suggestion. We should try and encourage juniors to play more tennis.

Effingham

Short(s) shrift

25 August 1989. In the context of the sunshine of 1989 and the mores of the 1990s, may men members please be permitted cool calves and ladies the right of tanned legs, by modernising the shorts and socks rule.

The Board, while accepting that the display of unclad male limbs of a fit man may give pleasure to the onlooker, nevertheless felt that this was perhaps outweighed by the effect of other less attractive underpinnings. With the campaign by the Prince of Wales for improved outward appearance of buildings in mind, it was the Board's opininon that if members or visitors wished to wear shorts on the course, it would be more decorus if they were worn with long stockings coming to just below the knee.

Rye

Luck of the draw

8 March 1990. I PROTEST – I may even rent a mob. The Club – the Committee – the Secretary – all of you. You deliberately flout the laws of chance. Not only do I have the same first round opponent as last time but I have him in both Founders and Parsons!

Sincere apologies from the computer on which the draw was made but the previous year's draw is not taken into consideration. The computer did comment that in fact you do not have the same opponent in the first rounds of the Parsons Putter and Family Foursomes. In the latter you have a bye into the second round and you will only play the same opponents if they are successful in the first round.

North Hants

Having slept on it

31 December 1977 [presumably late at night]. I suggest that the incumbent Committee resigns en masse.

2 January 1978 [presumably early in the morning]. I withdraw the preceding without reservation and offer my apology to my Committee.

Helensburgh

On second thoughts

I suggest

Anon.

Consideration for others

Members chewing gum on the links should keep their mouths shut and face away from the clubhouse.

Prestwick

Byes

Letter from The Secretary on 31 May 1936:

Lest the susceptibilities of our visitors, on whom we depend for support, be offended, the Committee asks me to request that your expression of disapproval at a shot not wholly successful may be couched in more moderate language than heretofore.

Royal Cromer

The Secretary, whilst regretting the absence of any Suggestion Book at his Club, said that he did receive suggestions from his members. However, contrary to popular belief, he did have a genuine birth certificate as did the Head Greenkeeper …

Royal Norwich

Finally …

Adult suggestions please!!

Anon.

The Ladies

Not popular

27 September 1898. We the undersigned members of the Cinque Ports Golf Club beg to protest most strongly against the admission of ladies to the links and clubhouse as we joined the Club under the distinct understanding that there were no lady members, and as there is no proper accommodation for them we would suggest that, should they desire to play, they should have their own links.

The Committee are of the opinion that the consideration of the question of providing ladies with a course and club rooms must be referred to the next Annual General Meeting.

Royal Cinque Ports

Early requests

10 November 1891. That a cloathes [*sic*] brush be provided.

A hand glass be provided.

Both agreed.

A long glass be provided to see petticoats.

There is no room for anything of the kind.

I suggest there should be a Club coat – red, with black collar and cuffs piped with white.

Agreed. It is recommended that black skirts and hats should be worn with it.

Royal Wimbledon

7 May 1905. That a looking glass (large one) & clock be provided in the only room in which ladies are permitted.

Rye

Tea time requests

1987. Any chance of a choice of larger tea cups (or mugs) as the first cup always tastes best!

Sorry but no.

June 1988. Any chance of having a kettle, jar of Nescafe / tea bag and a few cups so one can make a quick drink when it is not convenient for the staff to prepare one.

The Committee were not in favour of providing a kettle etc as the bar is always open and drinks can be obtained.

Tandridge Ladies

A brown study

23 May 1924. Is it necessary for the floor to be covered with brown paper on a Ladies match day even if it's a Friday.

Hale

Rights on and off the course

December 1910. That ladies should not be allowed to play on the North course on public holidays pending the passing of the Women's Suffrage Bill [sic]. Several ladies were playing today – a bank holiday.

This will not be allowed in future.

Burhill

27 March 1912. If a member is fortunate enough to be honoured by a lady's presence to lunch or tea, I suggest that he should, at least, be able to entertain her in the dining room (as at all civilised Golf Clubs I know of,

Sandwich etc) and not have to feed in a dirty little den adjoining the WCs.

The above can only be dealt with at the General Meeting as it entails an alteration in the Rules.

Royal Cinque Ports

14 May 1919. That, as during the period of hostilities, many privileges have been granted to ladies (e.g. the use of the smoking room, bar and lounge, and the relaxation of the old rule that mixed matches, or ladies matches, should not start before 11 a.m. on Saturdays and Sundays); and as they now seem to regard these privileges as rights, the time has now come to revert to the pre-war conditions: and notices should be placed on all doors leading to Men's quarters to keep the ladies in their proper part of the clubhouse.

Agreed.

Hunstanton

5 September 1922. That an official list of the ladies competition days be posted in a conspicuous position where the male members of the Club can see it. This would give the members a chance of going to Brancaster, or at any rate avoiding the morning round on these links.

5 September 1922. That on the days set apart for Ladies competition, the male members should not be compelled to play from LGU tees, and that, therefore, either fresh tee boxes be supplied for the ladies tees or else the Men's tee boxes be left in their normal places and the Ladies play from their LGU signposts. This would obviate the reduction of many of the holes to a farcical kindergarten length as was the case today.

Agreed.

Hunstanton

5 June 1961. I understand that the reason for the large premium the gentlemen members pay over that of ladies is to keep the course clear for men at weekends. Today four men's singles were held up by a lady being on the course at about 9 a.m. I would suggest that all lady members be reminded of the laws.

18 July 1971. That senior lady members be asked to observe the rules of golf when playing three balls and cutting in front of foursomes knockouts.

The Lady Captain has been notified of this incident.

Chislehurst

Pubic baths

February 1957. Could the steward be given the necessary powers to prevent the wives of members, temporary or otherwise, washing and drying their daughters' feet in front of the fire in the lounge? This was once a Golf Club.

Littlestone

Too crowded in the dining room

11 October 1908. That the presence of ladies in the luncheon room at mid-day and on the balcony is not conducive to the Club's welfare. [Signed by one member who added "and on behalf of various sympathising members too timid to sign their names"]

The objection has been noticed.

Seaford

What's in a name?

Is it true that as a compliment to our lady members the course is to be called Womenslow G.C.?

Wilmslow

More restrictions in the clubhouse

1992. Allowing ladies into the men's bar is a serious threat to the traditions of the Club.

Only permitted after 2.30 pm, to meet the need for a "spike bar" for afternoon mixed matches.

1993. Now the gallery bar is open, can the men's bar be brought back to men only?

Agreed.

Tandridge

We wish to suggest for the Committee's consideration that Ladies should be permitted the use of the Men's lounge and bar daily after 5.30 p.m. during the winter months.

Royal Wimbledon

Skirting round a problem

March 1977. As a full member of this golf course I take grave exception to being barred from the mixed lounge because I did not bring a jacket. I make the suggestion that the question of dress should apply also to the ladies and the juniors where golf apparel should not be worn in the lounge. I shall wear a jacket when ladies wear dresses.

The Committee's considered opinion is that the majority of members are satisfied with the rule as it stands.

Helensburgh

Flags in shreds – confuse the enemy!

7 April 1981. While watching our Bronze team playing on April 6th I was disgusted at the condition of the flags. Not only were they in shreds on some holes but on the front nine they were an assortment of yellow and white. Surely we can afford a matching set.

The Committee apologises and confirms that new tee and green furniture is in place.

Boyce Hill

The Nineteenth Hole

Those were the days

1894. That considering there is a difference of about 8/- a gallon in price between whisky and gin that gin should be only 4d and 2d per large and small glass respectively.

Members should bear in mind that no charge is made for attendance, use of linen etc. The profits now are so small that the Committee do not see their way to make any reduction.

It seems the answer to the previous suggestion rather begs the question. It is suggested that a charge of 1d be made for serviettes and so fall on the person using same and not that a drinker of a gin and ginger beer should pay more than the whisky and soda to provide for the washing-up.

Woking

September 1901. That the price of brandy and soda is too high. Precisely the same brandy and soda is supplied at the Queen's Club for 6d.

The price has now been lowered.

[Added comment by complainant] To 8d, still 2 pence more than the above.

Littlestone

1909. 3/6d for a small bottle (four glasses) of very inferior port, undecanted and muddy, is high when a much superior port is being sold at 6d a glass.

This will receive my immediate attention (H S Colt).

Sunningdale

April 1931. That the price of all drinks is reduced, beer should not be 10p per pint at the Club.

This matter will be looked into by the House Committee.

Saunton

The eternal quest

8 October 1932. The undersigned, having special interest in the quality of the draught beer supplied in the clubhouse, are of the opinion that the existing source of supply should be changed. The beer at present supplied is exceedingly bitter and unpalatable and no improvement has been observed despite repeated complaints which we understand have been brought to the notice of the brewers by the Committee.

18 October 1932. With reference to the suggestion dated 8 October 1932 the undersigned, being seasoned beer drinkers, are perfectly satisfied with the beer at present and consider that any change could be for the worse.

[To both] The Committee is dealing with the matter.

Porters Park

4 September 1985. Having suggested a change of bitter beer some years ago without success, may we repeat our appeal. We feel sure an examination of declining revenue from bitter beer sales will confirm that it is one of the most unpalatable drinks in the country.

Consideration is being given to this matter.

Royal Cinque Ports

9 October 1996. Could we look into stocking a really decent "real ale"? A local brew like Gales HSB for example. The Courage is apt to induce wind, the Boddington is metallic and the Adnams does not travel. It tastes quite different when delivered by a dray in Suffolk.

We endeavour to change beers on a regular basis so as to offer variety except for Adnams which is in constant demand. We acknowledge Adnams will not be exactly the same as when consumed locally in Suffolk.

Hankley Common

Please could you change your beers so that the members could have a decent drink?

Noted.

Royal North Devon

Gentlemen's Relish

31 December 1970. Owing to the lamentable lack of supplies of Gentlemen's Relish, may we please have toast and marmite rather than naked toast?

Prestwick

Better safe ...

25 March 1950. Could we have brandy in the bar please if only in case of illness.

Hale

Ah! Putting mixture

31 May 1959. That it would be in the interests of the Club that KUMMEL be on offer during the Spring Meeting. There seems little point in a mixed bar without it!

It is regretted that, due to an unexpectedly large sale of Kummel immediately prior to the Spring Meeting, the stock had run out and the wine merchants were unable to deliver in time. There is now, and will be in future, an ample stock of Kummel.

Chislehurst

The missing cherries at Royal Cinque Ports

6 July 1991. Could the Captain and Committee consider restoring the supply of cherries for our Pimms? – the lack of which is sorely missed.

After two hours of deliberation and a secret ballot the Committee voted by a narrow majority to agree to this very important request.

April 1994. After two hours of deliberation and a secret ballot in July 1991, the Committee agreed to restore the supplies of cherries for our Pimms. Could we respectfully suggest that a new jar be purchased for the benefit of all? (all?)

Of course – but a word of warning:

Pimms, Pimms, wonderful Pimms
Drink up, and always be merry
Just add what I say,
Ever keep it that way,
But please never put in a cherry!
James Pimm, Pimms Oyster Bar, London.

27 August 1955. Once again congratulations to the Captain, Committee, Secretary and his staff for providing us with yet another excellent Deal Week. Alas, the supply of cherries for our Pimms ran out – a tragic loss! Could consideration be given to increasing the supply post haste?

Your comments of appreciation of a highly successful Deal Week '95 were most welcome. Now to your concern of cherry shortage. This request was made in July 1991 and no further complaints were made of shortages until April 1994 (33 months). Now after 16 months a further complaint has been registered. The demand for cherries is undoubtedly increasing and these interesting statistics of cherry consumption/time will be put to the Chief Steward who will take swift action to remedy the problem. However, I refer to the comments (above) by James Pimm that cherries should not be taken with Pimms.

Royal Cinque Ports

A call for bigger bottles?

14 October 1965. Why should not the bar be furnished with a bottle cooler for largers [*sic*], tonic etc.?

This suggestion is accepted in principle and subject to the question of reasonable cost the provision of a cooler is being investigated.

Hindhead

Bar stocks

1 February 1974. The retiring members of the Committee suggest that the display of Smith's crisps be improved or discontinued.

In future potato crisps will be sold only in the professional's shop.

Porters Park

24 October 1994. The current selection of bar snacks (e.g. crisps and birdseed (peanuts)) is unimaginative and boring!! Please can we have some cheese snacks and nuts and raisins and something to make me more FAT!!

Anon.

Ice house needed

1897. No ice on July 14 – a very hot day.

No ice July 15.
No ice July 29.
Suggested that some notice be taken of suggestions or the suggestion book be abolished.

A continuous supply of ice has been ordered. Owing to the extreme heat of the last fortnight it has been found impossible to keep it, but it is hoped the supply will be sufficient in future.

Woking

For the want of a nail

Pre-1986. We need another bottle opener behind the bar.

Our resources do not stretch to employing another steward.

Hayling

Counted out

February 1966. An improved version of the pump for draught beer please. One pint should equal 10 seconds flat into the glass.
Signed thirsty Sassenachs ... and one beer-slurping Scot.

Yes.

Helensburgh

18 November 1989. We, the undersigned, would welcome the choice of a <u>damm good Burgundy</u> at

lunch. We are pleased to put our names forward as members of any proposed tasting committee.

Prestwick

10 August 1996. No scotch whisky!!!

Scotch whisky etc. was ordered on 31 July and enquiries have been made as to the cause of delay.

Woking

Levels of service

January 1898. I came in today and found nothing hot left. You can't expect a hypochondriac to eat a cold lunch and play golf on it!

Royal Ashdown Forest

30 September 1973. Now that we are introducing starting times for medal play, may we please have similar facilities for the reservation of "cottage pie" for lunch time?

Once the new microwave equipment has been installed in the kitchen, there should be no need to reserve cottage pie, or indeed any item on the Club's menu.

Walton Heath

Would it not be possible to put the rolls served at meals on Sundays in the oven for a suitable period. They would then be more palatable.

Agreed.

Royal Cinque Ports

1963. That an improvement is needed in the standard of meat carving at lunch.

Don't shoot the pianist – he's doing his best...

Tandridge

It is suggested that the Irish stew should have a touch of onion about it.

Noted.

Royal Cinque Ports

30 April 1933. That it should be possible for members and their guests who do not desire to, or are forbidden, to eat meat, to obtain fish or even a boiled egg in lieu thereof.

Whilst willing to meet the wishes of members the suggestion would impose too great a burden upon the kitchen and catering staff.

Porters Park

10 February 1990. Can a "HAPPY HOUR" be introduced (Friday p.m.)?

This did not find favour with the Committee.

Hayling

1 August 1939. We want treacle tart on Sundays.

Treacle tart is served as often as considered desirable.

Porters Park

9 January 1966. That on Sundays (and Saturdays) a certain amount of licence be permitted to regular drinkers in the bar regarding the times for luncheon, and should they be overduly hastened by importunate advances (inside the men's bar) of the kitchen staff.

This will be attended to.

Royal Cinque Ports

The little hut

10 April 1991. The Scene: The Halfway hut 11.00ish. It is crowded (for one reason and no other). In between serving 3 smoked salmon and Beluga in a bap, 2 Perrier (sorry, Aqua Libra) and 1 Costa Rican (freeze dried, no-nonsense 15 second percolated brup, bup, bop, bop, bip, kresweesch…!!!) coffee, a senior long standing member of the Club approaches the staff for service…

Customer: "4 cokes, 2 sausage on brown, 2 on white, thanks."

Staff: "Sorry but you'll have to wait until I've served the caddies out the back here."

The Customers (amid much laughter): "Well we'll just wait another 10 minutes or so until the next batch of Lincolnshire with dill, marjoram and golden thyme prize winning sausages are cooked to a mouth watering and succulent perfection ad bl—dy infinitum."

The only obvious conclusion from all this? Bring back Joyce please.

Anon.

5 December 1992. Could I suggest that Harry is allowed to sell cigarettes in the hut. I am sure that they could be taken backwards and forwards with the bottles of drink.

Suggestion accepted and implemented.

Royal Cinque Ports

15 June 1995. How about some fruit, nuts, and crisps in the halfway hut?

15 June 1995. Also regarding the halfway hut could we have some vegetarian sausages?

[Replies to both indecipherable]

Effingham

13 December 1995. Halfway Hut – 85p for a tea bag dropped into a miniscule paper cup filled with lukewarm water – another good example of value for money at the Club.

Anon.

More complaints

15 December 1994. After asking at the bar 19th for a pot

of tea for two and two slices of toast, I was told I should go to the cafe down the road by the Chef. I was quite civil and do not expect to be spoken to like that in such a rude manner. The chap I was playing with was also a member and was most embarrassed by this "cooling" outburst.

The Committee note and thank you for your comments. This matter is being dealt with by the Captain.

Epsom

3 May 1995. What has happened to the Coronation Chicken? Since when do you add salad to a curry?

Anon.

August 1998. Would it be possible for the bar to stay open on a Saturday night after 9.30 p.m. which, to my bewilderment, was when it shut yesterday. I was also shocked that I was asked to leave at this early hour.

[Signed: A Concerned Member]

Dear Concerned Member. I note the shock and bewilderment over the bar closing early and I will speak to the staff. However, in view that you reported this bar complaint in the Greens Suggestion book I feel that perhaps the bar had been open too long.

Thorpe Hall

16 April 1993. I ordered two bacon sandwiches they took half an hour to come and when they finally came the bacon was too well done and the bread was too thin.

Referred to the Secretary.

Epsom

This may damage your health

August 1901. That a better brand of Egyptian cigarettes be kept.

Littlestone

9 April. That "Virginia" cigarettes be supplied. Churchmans are good.

Refer to Refreshment Committee.

Hunstanton

March 1925. Mayan alternative Turkish cigarette to Abdullahs be supplied. They are expensive and nasty. Might the anglo-American Cigarette Company's "Kremlin" be given a trial? They are 9/- a 100.

Littlestone

Tea and coffee

February 1908. That "real" China tea be provided.

Good China tea is kept at the Club and provided if asked for.

Littlestone

1 December 1913. That some desirable coffee be procured instead of the present concoction of bitter herbs.

Formby

November 1952. That the specific gravity of afternoon tea be doubled.

Royal Wimbledon

July 1910. That as much tea and bread and butter etc. be obtainable for six pence as anyone desires.

This matter will receive attention.

Burhill

Not up to scratch (at Royal Wimbledon)

September 1932. The draft [*sic*] bitter is very unpalatable, I found it impossible to drink a half tankard to the end.

June 1936. The Club cheese is not what it was.

May 1952. That something be done to ensure that the supply of ice is equal to the demand in hot weather.

June 1952. No ice at 6 p.m. Still no ice at 1.30 p.m. or 6 p.m.

March 1963. May the Club wine list please be brought up to date? A few days ago I entertained guests from Muirfield offering them with some pride Crofts 1927. The wine turned out to be Crofts 1945, a great port as is known, but the equivalent of a generation adrift.

Royal Wimbledon

Various requests

1923. The fruit cake served up with tea is unpalatable.

This will be changed.

Sunningdale

January 1939. That it be possible to obtain "crumpet" for tea at weekends.

The answer is in the affirmative.

Chislehurst

May 1928. That when beef is purchased it should be sirloin with the undercut attached, and also that it should be English.

Only English beef is provided – sirloin is not considered a suitable joint for Club purposes.

Royal Ashdown Forest

14 May 1961. At a lunch costing 7/6, butter should be provided, not margarine.

This will be attended to.

Aldeburgh

2 May 1961. I would suggest that hot sausages be served at the bar in the evenings. The hotplate could be heated by candles at very little expense and the sausages not eaten could be served next day cold.

Hot snacks not approved but cold snacks will be available.

Seacroft

15 January 1967. I understand that the Club has an electric kettle. May this please be installed in the bar so that the discriminating who enjoy hot whisky and lemon may do so with boiling water rather than lukewarm water?

The Committee is very sympathetic with your request but suggest that the matter be postponed until more staff is available. The House Committee is working on the staff problem now and any delay should only be of a temporary nature.

Hindhead

22 September 1972. Would the House Committee consider the possibility of providing a second green vegetable at luncheon, at times when broad beans appear on the menu. It is not disputed that broad beans are an excellent vegetable and of great nutritional value, however I am sure there is a sizeable minority of members in the Club who would like to see a choice of vegetables on the menu, when the aforesaid beans appear thereon.

We are examining ways of introducing more variety into our luncheon menus and hope to be able to offer a wider choice of vegetables in the near future.

Walton Heath

15 May 1976. That the present apologia for tonic water be replaced by "Schweppes" …Schw……(you know who).

Noted. Steward informed.

Royal Cinque Ports

May 1992. Could there be a little more flexibility on sandwiches for tea. The present selection is <u>very</u> limited. Surely tomato, cheese, or cucumber would not stretch things too much – and are more in keeping with a tea menu than ham.

Anon.

Screen test fails

12 March 1987. I suggest that the screens in the dining room should be removed for the following reasons:

1. They spoil what was a pleasant room.
2. They reduce the light and outlook in the dining room.

3. They separate members from each other and give a feeling of claustrophobia.

If it is essential to separate those 'improperly dressed' from the rest then 3 or 4 tables or perhaps one long table could be set aside at one end of the room <u>without</u> screens.

The Executive Committee considered the points you make but, on balance, are satisfied that the dining room screens have proved to be advantageous to both members and visitors during busy lunchtime periods. The screens will therefore remain.

Anon.

Sexist

3 January 1973. That a plain omelette always be available at lunch, consisting of 3 eggs for a man and 2 eggs for a woman.

The Chef will always prepare an omelette on request, but there may be some slight delay whenever the dining room is particularly busy.

Walton Heath

Other culinary concerns

14 May 1991. Would the chef's time be better employed doing something other than making greasy chips??

15 May 1991. The taste of grease would seem to me to indicate that it has been used previously and therefore could be carcinogenic. Please have this checked, by competent medical analysis. Thanks.

Anon.

21 June 1999. [Suggestion from junior member] I suggest that pork pies should be sold on a regular basis as they are very nice and fulfil my hunger substantially. PS The price should also be cut to a reasonable price.

Scarborough North Cliff

Not got a light?

10 June 1994. If the bar is to sell cigars singly, the bar staff should be able to provide a light. It should not be necessary to buy a box of matches in these circumstances. In the past I have provided matches to be placed behind the bar. These were stolen! Could the Club afford to provide a future supply please?

The Committee do not support your suggestion. Matches are on sale behind the bar and therefore all smokers are able to purchase the necessary items to enjoy a "light up". The problem could further be solved by the purchase of a lighter to be kept in one's possession!

North Hants

Breathe in the tube, please

21 October 1967. That the Club purchase a breathalyser.

Under investigation.

Saunton

Champagne foresight

In the hope that we will be holding a really top class dance for our Centenary in 1984, would the Committee consider purchasing 10 cases of champagne now, whilst the price is c.£6 per bottle. There is a) a shortage of supply in France and b) the Americans are beginning to buy much more. Prices will inevitably rise soon.

Thank you for the suggestion. This has been referred to the House and Wine Committee.

Aldeburgh

Finally, a double disaster

January 1968. No Club stilton. Females at every table.
Royal Wimbledon

Dare we look into the Suggestion Book of the future?

June 2201. Update history of Club.

January 2286. Extend course lease to February 2586.
Royal Wimbledon

A Bye

The following poem appeared in 1895, about a year after the Helensburgh Golf Club was formed.

OUR GOLF CLUB

We have a goodish golfing course
Right up the Luss Road hill;
Small matter that the players there
To climb must have a will.

We have a house of shelter too,
Where keep we clubs and clothes;
What matter then if on the links
It rains, or snows, or blows?

We have some fairish teeing grounds,
Where one can steady stand;
What does it matter then if some
Have slopes superbly grand.

We have a putting green or two,
Whereon the ball can run;
What signifies if on the rest
No putting can be done?

We have a large directorate,
Composed of active men;
What matters it, if like the gods,
They nod, sir, now and then.

We have a Secretary bold,
Indeed a man of mettle;
Small matter that he fails to tell
Accounts are still to settle.

We play a medal round or two,
It helps the hand and eye;
What matters if the scoring cards
Long in the box should lie?

We have a book of handicaps,
Where hopes and fears are centred;
Small matter though for four long months
Naught therein's been entered.

We hold a meeting once a year,
We hear the Chairman's voice;
What matter though he praises all?
It makes their hearts rejoice.

And all the men elect again,
They promise to improve;
No matter if they find it stiff
To quit the grand old groove.

So let us sing, long live the king,
The Club, and every member;
And let us live, in peace and love,
Until, well, next December.

*This elicited a strong equally critical letter in the press,
followed shortly afterwards with this poetic reply.*

OUR GOLF CLUB: A RETURN MATCH

Who says our links are on a hill?
That climbing thereward makes one ill?
The Club to pay the doctor's bill.
Small matter.

Who says our house keeps clubs and clothes
From summer's rain, from winter's snow?
A place, in fact, to toast one's toes –
And chatter.

Who thinks we have no proper tee
For afternoons? For driving free?
That this is not what ought to be.
No matter.

Who speaks about a putting green?
Perhaps a putter ne'er has seen,
May on a link have never been.
What matter.

Who blames our large directorate,
For rushing blindly to their fate,
By nods the gods might emulate?
Sad matter.

Who says our Secretary bold,
Does everything but what he's told?
Such men are worth their weight in gold.
Great matter.

Who fancies every handicap,
Should be like bitter beer – on tap?
Thinks scoring cards are used for nap.
Pure patter.

Who deems the worthy in the chair,
Was far too friendly to be fair?
Much better to have pulled their hair,
Than flatter.

Who thinks Committee can't improve,
Themselves from out the same old groove?
Would all the men, in fact, remove.
Mere clatter.

And so the lines to end to bring,
Suggests that all who can should sing –
Long life to our prospective king.
Then scatter.

Index to the Clubs Included